How to Use

History Pockets

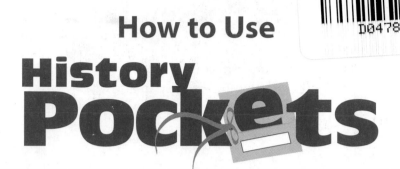

In *History Pockets—Ancient Greece,* students explore the amazing civilization that gave us democracy, the Olympics, and the Parthenon. The engaging activities are stored in labeled pockets and bound into a decorative cover. Students will be proud to see their accumulated projects presented all together. At the end of the book, evaluation sheets have been added for teacher use.

Make a Pocket

1. Use a 12" x 18" (30.5 x 45.5 cm) piece of construction paper for each pocket. Fold up 6" (15 cm) to make a 12" (30.5 cm) square.

2. Staple the right side of each pocket closed.

3. Punch two or three holes in the left side of each pocket.

Assemble the Pocket Book

1. Reproduce the cover illustration on page 3 for each student.

2. Direct students to color and cut out the illustration and glue it onto a 12" (30.5 cm) square of construction paper to make the cover.

3. Punch two or three holes in the left side of the cover.

4. Fasten the cover and the pockets together. You might use string, ribbon, twine, raffia, or binder rings.

Every Pocket Has...

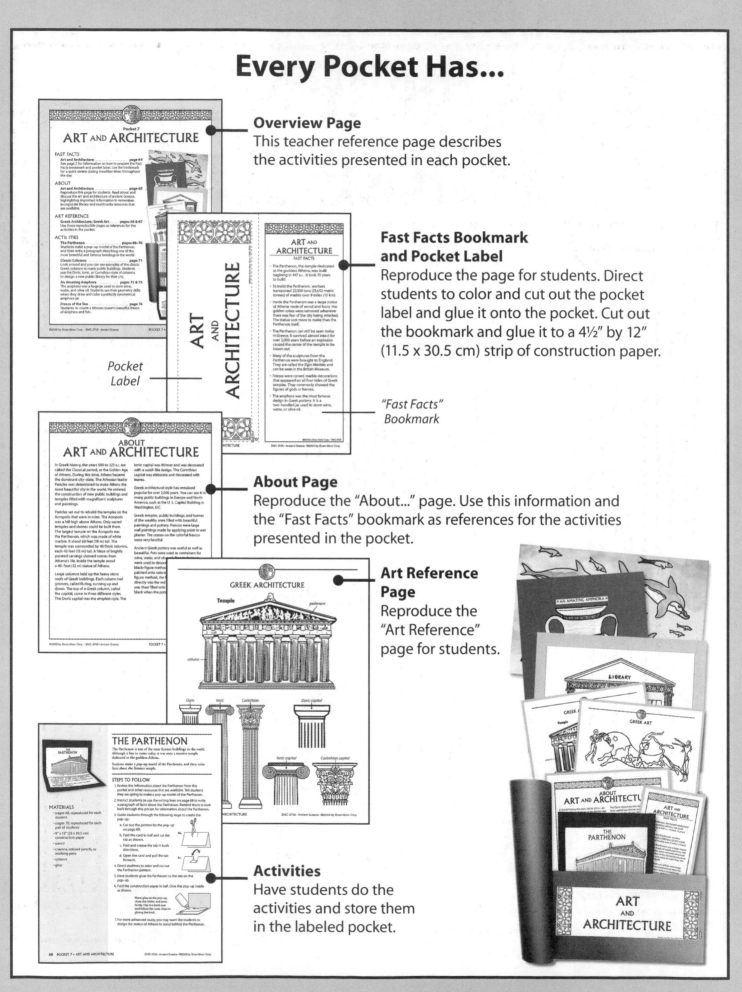

Overview Page
This teacher reference page describes the activities presented in each pocket.

Pocket Label

Fast Facts Bookmark and Pocket Label
Reproduce the page for students. Direct students to color and cut out the pocket label and glue it onto the pocket. Cut out the bookmark and glue it to a 4½" by 12" (11.5 x 30.5 cm) strip of construction paper.

"Fast Facts" Bookmark

About Page
Reproduce the "About..." page. Use this information and the "Fast Facts" bookmark as references for the activities presented in the pocket.

Art Reference Page
Reproduce the "Art Reference" page for students.

Activities
Have students do the activities and store them in the labeled pocket.

EMC 3705 • Ancient Greece • ©2003 by Evan-Moor Corp.

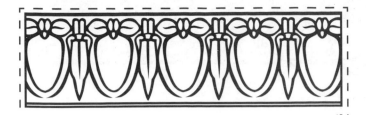

INTRODUCTION TO
ANCIENT GREECE

ANCIENT GREECE
FAST FACTS

- Ancient Greeks would be surprised if you called them by that name. Their name for their civilization was *Hellas*. Greek-speaking people were called Hellenes.

- The geography of Greece is unique. There is a mainland that is 365 miles (587 km) long and 343 miles (552 km) wide. Then there are over 2,000 islands that are all part of Greece.

- Mount Olympus is the highest mountain peak in Greece. The ancient Greeks believed Zeus, king of the gods, lived there with his family of gods and goddesses.

- The ancient Greeks lived on or near the Ionian, the Aegean, and the Mediterranean Seas.

- The Greek philosopher Plato believed that a civilization called Atlantis had existed on an island near Greece and that it disappeared into the ocean.

- The Mycenaeans conquered the Minoans in 1450 B.C. The war-like Mycenaean people lived on the mainland of Greece. Their soldiers wore complete bronze-plated suits with boar-tusk helmets.

ABOUT
ANCIENT GREECE

Ancient Greece has been called the "birthplace of Western Civilization." European culture was greatly influenced by the Greeks. The areas of art, literature, history, philosophy, politics, and science all had their roots in ancient Greece.

The area in which the ancient Greeks lived was centered in the Aegean Sea. Ancient Greece was not one country with a single ruler or government. It was a collection of small independent city-states.

The history of ancient Greece can be divided into periods or ages.

PERIOD OR AGE (DATES)	IMPORTANT FACTS
Early Period or Bronze Age (3000 B.C. to 1100s B.C.)*	• Minoan and the Mycenaean civilizations • built cities with palaces high on hilltops • large fleets of ships • had a system of writing • both cultures collapsed because of warfare and volcanic eruptions
Dark Ages (1100 B.C. to 800 B.C.)	• individual, isolated city-states made up of a large city and its surrounding land
Archaic Period (800 B.C. to 480 B.C.)	• started to trade with other nations • city-states grew more powerful • Athens and Sparta dominant • set up colonies in the Mediterranean Sea
Classical Age (480 B.C. to 323 B.C.)	• great burst of culture • the first democracy • great works of architecture, art, and drama
Hellenistic Age (323 B.C. to 30 B.C.)	• Philip of Macedonia defeated the Greeks • Philip united all of Greece • Alexander the Great ruled after Philip • Alexander extended Greek rule from Egypt to India

After Alexander the Great died, native warlords controlled ancient Greece. Then the Romans invaded. They conquered Greece in 146 B.C. The Romans admired the Greek culture and adopted many cultural aspects of it.

Greece did not become an independent nation again until the early 1800s.

*All dates on this chart are approximate.

MACEDONIA

THRACE

Mount Olympus ▲

THESSALY

Troy

AEGEAN
SEA

LYDIA

Thermopylae

Delphi

ATTICA

Thebes

Marathon
Athens

Mycenae

Piraeus

PELOPONNESUS

Salamis

Olympia

Cos

Sparta

IONIAN
SEA

MEDITERRANEAN
SEA

CRETE

N

MAP OF
ANCIENT
GREECE

MATERIALS

- pages 8 and 9, reproduced for each student
- pencil
- colored pencils
- scissors
- glue or transparent tape

STEPS TO FOLLOW

1. As a class, discuss the importance of historical time lines. Ask students to look through reference materials to see different ways important events are recorded on time lines. As students read about ancient Greece, they will record important dates and events on their own time lines.

2. Hand out pages 8 and 9 and discuss what is already on the ancient Greece time line.

3. Have students cut out the time line sections on pages 8 and 9.

4. Instruct students to assemble the time line by gluing or taping the three pieces together.

5. Tell students they will add important dates, pictures, and short explanations of events chosen throughout the unit.

6. Fold the time line in half and store it in Pocket 1.

ANCIENT GREECE TIME LINE

Students are about to travel back in time to ancient Greece. The period lasted from approximately 2000 B.C. to 146 B.C.

As students learn about the people and events of this exciting era, they will add important dates, pictures, and short explanations to a time line. The first and last entries have been done for them, and there are hints in between to help students along the way.

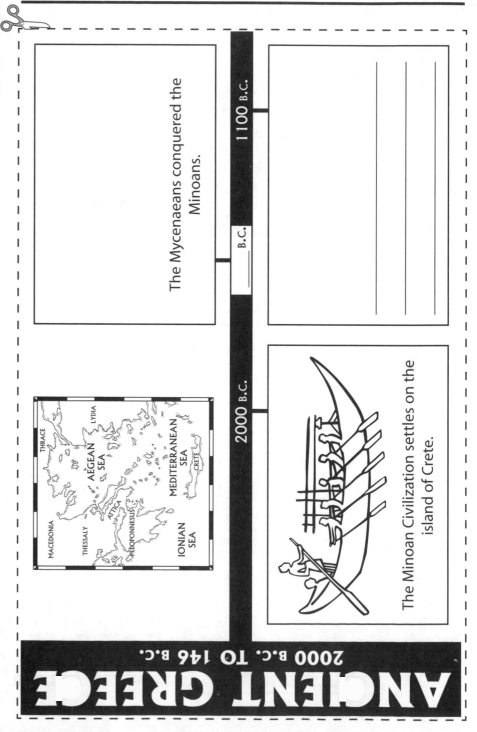

   EMC 3705 • Ancient Greece • ©2003 by Evan-Moor Corp.

⊞ ANCIENT GREECE TIME LINE ⊞

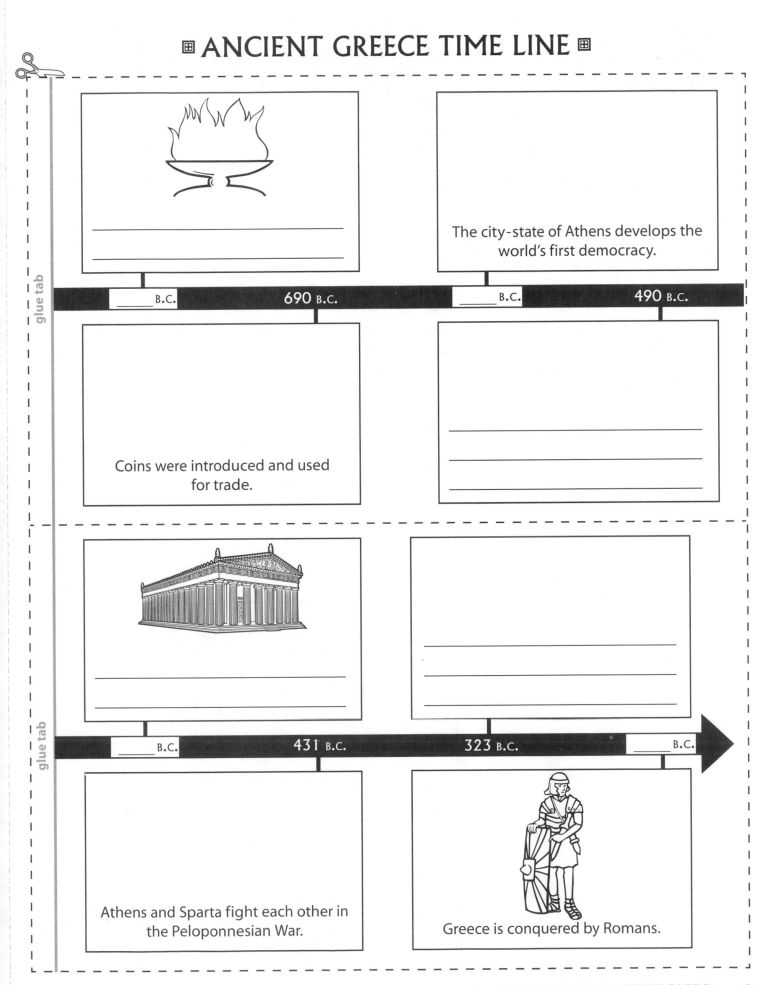

The city-state of Athens develops the world's first democracy.

| _____ B.C. | 690 B.C. | _____ B.C. | 490 B.C. |

Coins were introduced and used for trade.

| _____ B.C. | 431 B.C. | 323 B.C. | _____ B.C. |

Athens and Sparta fight each other in the Peloponnesian War.

Greece is conquered by Romans.

glue tab

glue tab

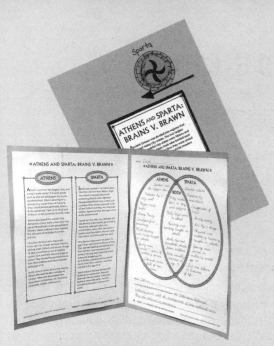

ATHENS AND SPARTA: BRAINS v. BRAWN

Students learn about the similarities and differences between the two rival city-states Athens and Sparta. Students can decide for themselves which city-state could have ruled all of ancient Greece.

STEPS TO FOLLOW

1. Read and discuss the information about Athens and Sparta on the bottom of this page and page 11.

2. Have students compare and contrast the two cultures using the Venn diagram on page 12.

3. Have students fold the construction paper in half. Glue the title and introductory paragraph on the front; glue pages 11 and 12 on the inside pages.

4. Illustrate the cover if desired.

5. Students then decide which city-state they think could have ruled all of ancient Greece. You may want to tally how many votes each one receives.

6. Optional: Divide the class into two groups—the Athenians and the Spartans. Have the two groups prepare a panel presentation or debate stating the reasons why their city-state is superior.

MATERIALS

- information on the bottom of this page, reproduced for each student
- pages 11 and 12, reproduced for each student
- pencil
- 12" x 18" (30.5 x 45.5 cm) construction paper
- glue
- Optional: crayons, marking pens, or colored pencils

ATHENS AND SPARTA: BRAINS v. BRAWN

Ancient Greece was divided into regions that contained many city-states. The two largest and most powerful city-states were Athens and Sparta. They were keen rivals who battled each other for power. The only time they were united was when they had to defeat outside invaders like the Persians.

Name: _____

EMC 3705 • Ancient Greece • ©2003 by Evan-Moor Corp.

ATHENS AND SPARTA: BRAINS v. BRAWN

Athens, a port on the Aegean Sea, was a major trade center. It traded goods such as olive oil and grapes for much-needed wheat. Athens developed a strong navy. Large fleets of fighting ships called triremes defended Athens. A city wall almost 7 feet (2 m) thick and 23 feet (7 m) tall protected the city-state.

Athens developed the world's first democracy. Every male citizen over the age of 18 took part in the government. Women, slaves, and men born outside the city were all excluded from this process.

Education for boys was important. From age 7 to 12 boys learned reading, writing, math, history, and music. At age 18, they served two years of military service. Girls were not allowed to go to school. They learned household chores from their mothers and often married at the age of 15.

As the cultural center of ancient Greece, Athens attracted the best artists and scholars. Athenians developed new ideas about architecture, art, literature, philosophy, politics, and science.

Sparta was located in an inland valley 150 miles (241 km) from Athens. High mountains formed a natural wall protecting the city-state. Spartans disapproved of trade and contact with outsiders. Male citizens received a plot of land to farm, but they also had to be soldiers. Sparta had the strongest army in the ancient world.

Sparta was the only city-state that did not develop a democratic government. Two kings, who were also army commanders, led it. Only men born in Sparta could be citizens. Women were not citizens, but they could own land.

Only Spartan boys were educated. At age 7, boys were sent to military school. They learned reading and writing, but the emphasis was on physical and military training. Boys had to be in the army until at least age 30. As in Athens, girls learned household chores from their mothers and often married at the age of 15.

Sparta was not famous for beautiful buildings or works of art because Spartans did not believe in luxuries. Sparta is remembered for its army, considered the best in the ancient world.

Name: _____

⊞ ATHENS AND SPARTA: BRAINS v. BRAWN ⊞

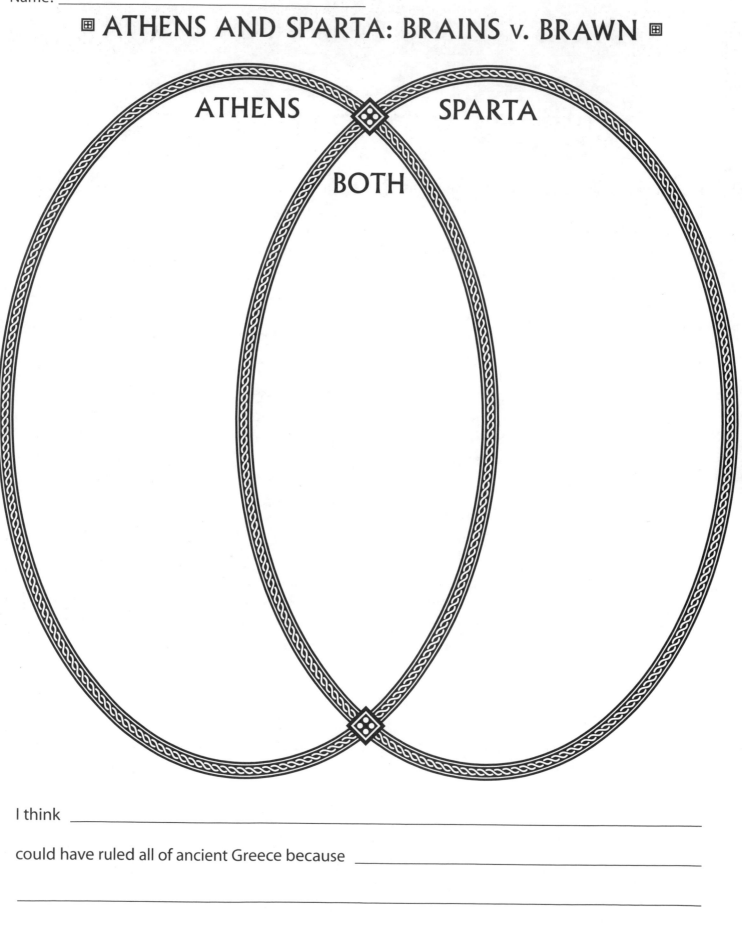

ATHENS

SPARTA

BOTH

I think _____

could have ruled all of ancient Greece because _____

_____

_____ .

EMC 3705 • Ancient Greece • ©2003 by Evan-Moor Corp.

MILITARY POWER

FAST FACTS

Military Power . . . . **page 14**
See page 2 for information on how to prepare the Fast
Facts bookmark and pocket label. Use the bookmark
for a quick review during transition times throughout
the day.

ABOUT

Military Power . . . . **page 15**
Reproduce this page for students. Read about
and discuss the military power of ancient Greece,
highlighting important information to remember.
Incorporate library and multimedia resources that
are available.

ART REFERENCE

Greek Military Equipment . . . . **page 16**
Use this reproducible page as a reference for the
activities in the pocket. Have students use information
found in this pocket to write captions for each
illustration.

ACTIVITIES

Winning the Persian Wars . . . . **pages 17 & 18**
Athens and Sparta joined forces to defeat the Persians.
One of their best defenses was the great warship
called the trireme. Have students follow the directions
on page 18 to make a booklet about Greek warfare.

Make Hoplite Shields . . . . **page 19**
Hoplites were elite foot soldiers who carried
fierce-looking shields. Students design a hoplite
shield to fit their personalities.

Alexander the Great . . . . **pages 20 & 21**
Alexander the Great was a military genius who
became the leader of the largest empire the world had
ever known. He was recognized for his intelligence
and courage. Students make a pennant as a tribute to
this great man.

MILITARY POWER

MILITARY POWER
FAST FACTS

- As part of their training, soldiers had to practice running in full armor. A suit of armor weighed as much as 66 pounds (30 kg).

- A chariot driver drove Athenian cavalry officers to the battle so they could shout orders and get a better view of the battle.

- After a victory, Greek soldiers hung their weapons in trees as offerings to the gods.

- Greeks used a heavy wooden beam, called a battering ram, to smash into walls. The battering ram got its name from the bronze ram-shaped head on the beam.

- To get over the wall of a city, armies used siege towers, gigantic wooden structures on wheels. The soldiers worked their way up inside the structure to the tallest platform so they could scale the walls.

- During the Mycenaean period, Greece fought the Trojan War against the city of Troy. An epic poem written by the Greek poet Homer told about this war. Students of history read the *Iliad* even today.

- Alexander the Great was only 20 years old when he conquered all of Greece, Asia Minor, Egypt, Persia, Syria, and Mesopotamia.

ABOUT
MILITARY POWER

Warfare was common in ancient Greece. Many internal and external conflicts led the Greeks to develop sophisticated armies and navies.

Even though the city-states were often bitter rivals, they did unite when a foreign invader threatened the whole region. The Persians led numerous attempts to control ancient Greece. Athens and Sparta joined forces to battle them. The Persian Wars were won with the combined might of Sparta's army and the Athenian navy.

After the Persian Wars, Athens headed an alliance called the Delian League, formed to protect Greece from further Persian invasions. Sparta, part of an alliance of the southern city-states, felt threatened by Athens' power. Sparta and her allies told Athens to loosen her control or go to war. When Athens refused, the Peloponnesian War began in 431 B.C.

The war lasted almost 30 years, with each side winning battles. Finally, Sparta won the war when the Persians provided Sparta with a fleet of ships. The Spartans destroyed Athens' fleet and then attacked Athens. The Athenians, forced to stay behind the city walls, were starved into surrendering in 404 B.C.

The Peloponnesian War left the whole empire in a weakened state. Philip II of Macedonia, a country north of Greece, seized control of the region. In 336 B.C. King Philip II was assassinated, and his son Alexander took control. Alexander the Great was not satisfied with just controlling Greece. He set off with his troops on a 20,000-mile (32,187 km) journey to conquer Egypt and the entire Persian Empire. During the next 13 years, Alexander created the largest empire in the Western world.

After Alexander's death in 323 B.C., his generals split up his empire. The region of Greece came under the control of warlords who were not united. Ancient Greece became vulnerable to outside conquest. The Romans saw the opportunity and invaded Greece. In 146 B.C. Greece became a province of Rome.

GREEK MILITARY EQUIPMENT

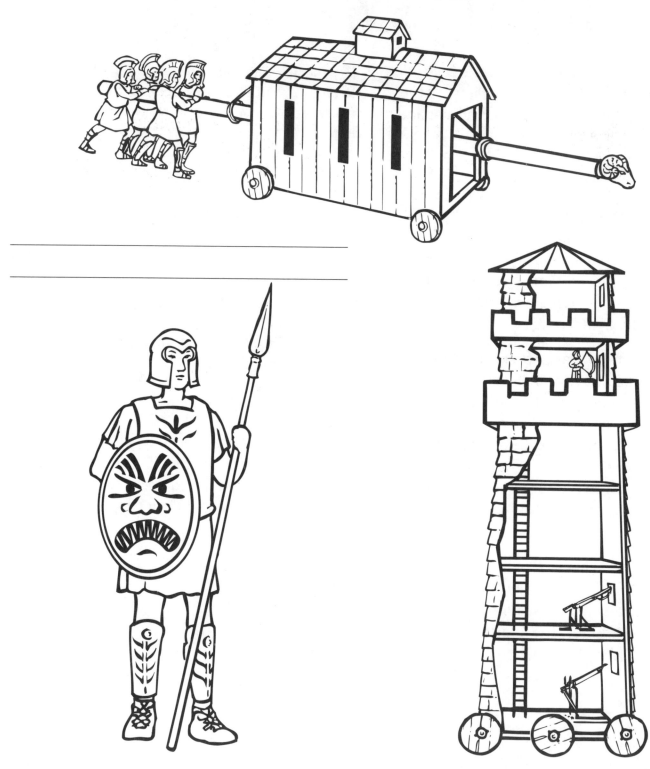

▣ WINNING THE PERSIAN WARS ▣

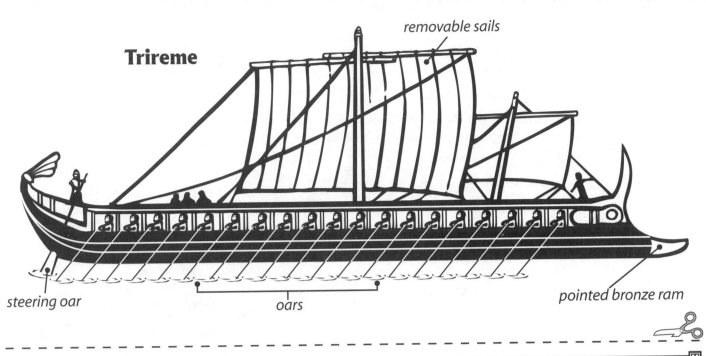

Trireme

removable sails

steering oar

oars

pointed bronze ram

Athens and Sparta, often enemies, joined forces to win a series of wars against the Persians. The Persians had wanted to extend their empire to include parts of ancient Greece.

In 499 B.C. Athens sent soldiers to help other city-states fight off a Persian invasion. They fought for five years, and finally Athenian forces defeated the Persians. The Persians invaded again in 490 B.C. In the Battle of Marathon, the Greeks were heavily outnumbered, but were able to defeat the Persians. Another battle took place in a narrow mountain pass. A small army of Greeks was able to hold back the Persians for a time. But the enemy found a way around the pass, marched into Athens, and set the city on fire.

The next major battle of the Persian Wars was a sea battle. In the Battle of Salamis, the Greeks tricked the Persians into believing the Greek ships were retreating. As the Persian fleet prepared to attack, the Greeks reversed their course and attacked first. They surrounded the Persian ships and rammed them. About 200 Persian ships were sunk, while the Greeks lost only 40 ships.

The Persians invaded one more time. The Greek army, led by the Spartans, defeated the Persians on land. Meanwhile, the Greek navy attacked and burned the entire Persian fleet of ships. Finally, in 479 B.C. the Persian invasion was over.

The Greeks could not have defeated their enemies without the great ships called triremes (trī rēmz).

⊞ WINNING THE PERSIAN WARS ⊞

STEPS TO FOLLOW

1. Read the information about the Persian Wars and the fast ships that helped the Greeks win the battles.

2. On the top half of a 12" x 18" (30.5 x 45.5 cm) piece of white construction paper, draw and color a side view of a trireme. Use the model on page 17 to help you.

3. Label your drawing as the model is labeled.

4. Cut out the two information boxes and glue them to the bottom of the paper.

5. Fold the paper in half to make a booklet. Color, cut out, and glue the trireme from page 17 to the cover.

6. Add the title "Winning the Persian Wars."

7. You may wish to add additional details to your booklet.

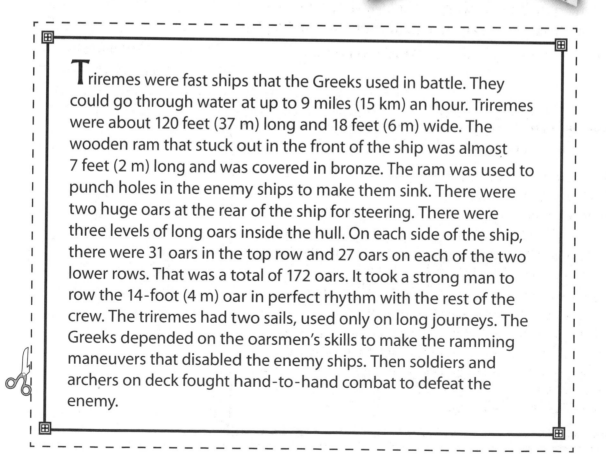

Triremes were fast ships that the Greeks used in battle. They could go through water at up to 9 miles (15 km) an hour. Triremes were about 120 feet (37 m) long and 18 feet (6 m) wide. The wooden ram that stuck out in the front of the ship was almost 7 feet (2 m) long and was covered in bronze. The ram was used to punch holes in the enemy ships to make them sink. There were two huge oars at the rear of the ship for steering. There were three levels of long oars inside the hull. On each side of the ship, there were 31 oars in the top row and 27 oars on each of the two lower rows. That was a total of 172 oars. It took a strong man to row the 14-foot (4 m) oar in perfect rhythm with the rest of the crew. The triremes had two sails, used only on long journeys. The Greeks depended on the oarsmen's skills to make the ramming maneuvers that disabled the enemy ships. Then soldiers and archers on deck fought hand-to-hand combat to defeat the enemy.

MAKE HOPLITE SHIELDS

Hoplites were elite foot soldiers. Students design their own shields to take into battle.

STEPS TO FOLLOW

1. With the class, read the information about the hoplites and their armaments.

2. Explain to students that hoplites wanted to intimidate their enemies, so the designs on their shields were fierce-looking. Designs such as scorpions, horses, sharks, gorgons, and sea monsters were common.

3. Have students design shields that reflect their own personalities. They draw the designs on the back (bottom) of the paper plate.

4. Instruct students to color their shield designs using bright primary colors.

5. Have students cut out the information and glue it to the front side of the plate.

6. Have students fold the tagboard strip to make a handle, as shown. Students glue the handle to the front side of the plate.

7. Encourage students to share their creations in class.

MATERIALS

- information below, reproduced for each student

- white or light yellow dinner-size paper plate (avoid plastic-coated plates)

- 2" x 8" (5 x 20 cm) strip of tagboard

- pencil

- marking pens

- scissors

- glue

HOPLITE SOLDIERS

Hoplites were elite foot soldiers. For protection a hoplite soldier wore a cuirass (a bronze and leather plate for the breast and back) and a bronze helmet adorned with horsehair crests. On his lower legs, a soldier wore guards called greaves. The hoplite carried a bronze and leather shield, a long spear, and a short iron sword.

Hoplite soldiers fought in a formation called a phalanx, a long block of soldiers that were eight ranks deep. If a man were killed, the soldier behind him would take his place. The shields of the soldiers formed a wall that protected them. The hoplite soldier's prized possession was his shield. Each hoplite was able to choose a unique design for his shield—the scarier the better.

ALEXANDER THE GREAT

Alexander the Great was a military genius who ruled the largest empire in the Western world. Alexander conquered many regions and set up numerous Greek cities along the way. Wherever he went, Alexander was treated with both respect and fear.

Students read about Alexander the Great and his mighty conquests. Then they pay tribute to this great man when they make a pennant in his honor.

MATERIALS

- page 21, reproduced for each student
- 9" x 12" (23 x 30.5 cm) white construction paper
- scraps of colored construction paper
- colorful construction paper streamers
- pencil
- crayons or marking pens
- glue

STEPS TO FOLLOW

1. Read and discuss the information about Alexander the Great.

2. Tell students that they are to design a pennant in honor of Alexander.

3. Have students fold and cut the construction paper as shown to make a triangular pennant.

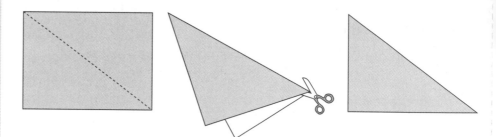

4. Direct them to write "Alexander the Great" and other words that describe him on the pennant.

5. Then students add designs and pictures that represent his life. His beloved horse, Bucephalus, is a picture that students may want to include.

6. Students may also want to add colorful streamers to the pennant.

⊞ ALEXANDER THE GREAT ⊞

Alexander the Great was one of the most famous military leaders the world has ever known. Alexander's father, King Philip, turned his kingdom of Macedonia into a great military power. He controlled Greece and wanted to conquer the Persian Empire. Before this ambition could be fulfilled, King Philip was assassinated. Thus, in 336 B.C., at the age of 20, Alexander took control of his father's kingdom and set out to fulfill his father's dream.

With 30,000 foot soldiers and 5,000 horsemen, Alexander, riding his beloved horse Bucephalus, left Macedonia on a 2,000-mile (3,219 km) journey of conquest. His army invaded the Persian Empire, where Alexander defeated the Persian king Darius III in a long and bloody battle. Darius, however, escaped.

His troops marched south toward Egypt. The Egyptians, thankful to be free of Persian rule, crowned Alexander pharaoh. Alexander built a city in the Nile Delta and named it Alexandria after himself.

Alexander next led his army into Persia. He captured the fabled city of Babylon and once again defeated Darius. When Darius was killed, Alexander declared himself king of Asia.

Alexander's thirst for control led him on another conquest. This time he set out to conquer India. The army traveled as far east as the Indus River, battling an Indian king whose army rode battle elephants. After months of fighting, heat, and rain, Alexander's army refused to go on. Alexander returned to Babylon in 323 B.C. There he became ill with a fever and died at the age of 33.

Alexander the Great was one of the greatest generals of all time, conquering lands from Egypt to India. Along the way, he built Greek cities and introduced Greek culture to the lands he conquered.

Pocket 3
DAILY LIFE

FAST FACTS

Daily Life . . . . **page 23**
See page 2 for information on how to prepare the Fast Facts bookmark and pocket label. Use the bookmark for a quick review during transition times throughout the day.

ABOUT

Daily Life . . . . **page 24**
Reproduce this page for students. Read about and discuss the daily life of ancient Greece, highlighting important information to remember. Incorporate library and multimedia resources that are available.

ART REFERENCE

A Greek Home . . . . **page 25**
Use this reproducible page as a reference for the activities in the pocket.

ACTIVITIES

Mosaic Tiles . . . . **page 26**
The art of mosaic was developed in ancient Greece. Small pieces of cut stone or glass were placed into a bed of plaster to create a beautiful mosaic tile. Students design and create their own mosaic tile to decorate a floor in their own homes.

A Greek Wedding . . . . **pages 27–29**
Weddings were cause for much celebration in ancient Greece. Students read about this tradition, noting the similarities and differences of a marriage ceremony in ancient Greece to a traditional one today. Students make an invitation to a Greek wedding.

A Game of Knucklebones . . . . **pages 30–31**
Games were part of everyday life for the ancient Greeks. Women and children played Knucklebones, a game using animal bones. Students make and then play a game of Knucklebones.

  EMC 3705 • Ancient Greece • ©2003 by Evan-Moor Corp.

DAILY LIFE

DAILY LIFE

FAST FACTS

- A typical house was built around a central courtyard. Doors to each room of the house faced the courtyard.

- When families ate together, the women and children sat on stools. Men reclined on couches to eat.

- Men spent a lot of time away from home. However, they did do all the grocery shopping, since women were rarely seen in public.

- Women were expected to stay home and manage the finances, food, housework, and take care of the children. Richer women had servants to help them.

- Both men and women wore hats to protect themselves from the sun. Having a suntan was not considered attractive.

- Children played with yo-yos, spinning tops, and hoops. Babies were given rattles and dolls.

- Favorite pets included birds, tortoises, and mice. Every family had a pet goat that gave them milk and cheese.

ABOUT
DAILY LIFE

Daily life in ancient Greece was very different for men and women. Men had much more freedom. Women led very sheltered lives, devoted to the home and the family.

The Greeks had small families. Boys were more valued because they would become the next citizens of the city-state. Girls could not become citizens. They left home at age 14 or 15 to get married.

Until the age of about 7, boys and girls were brought up at home. Children played with yo-yos, spinning tops, and hoops. Boys were expected to go to school at age 7. The purpose of education was to create good citizens to take part in running the government. Girls remained at home, learning from their mothers, until they married.

Most people lived in one- or two-story houses built around a courtyard. The mud-brick and plaster houses had gently sloping roofs covered with clay tiles. Larger houses had a small kitchen, a room for bathing, a men's dining room, and a women's sitting area. Women and children lived separately from the men in larger homes.

A typical meal included bread, fish, goat cheese, and vegetables such as lentils, leeks, and onions. For dessert, Greeks loved almonds, figs, apples, grapes, and pomegranates. On special occasions, they ate meat cooked in olive oil and garlic. Wine mixed with water was the Greeks' favorite drink.

Men, women, and children wore simple rectangular woolen or linen tunics called chitons. A woolen outer cloth called a himation was then wrapped around the body like a cloak. Adults and children went barefoot indoors and wore leather sandals when outdoors. Both men and women wore hats to prevent a suntan. Pale skin was a sign of true beauty. Greeks bathed regularly and rubbed olive oil onto their skin to keep it soft. Beauty and cleanliness were very important.

Storytelling and music were also important in the daily lives of the ancient Greeks. The Greeks also believed that dance improved both physical and emotional health.

EMC 3705 • Ancient Greece • ©2003 by Evan-Moor Corp.

A GREEK HOME

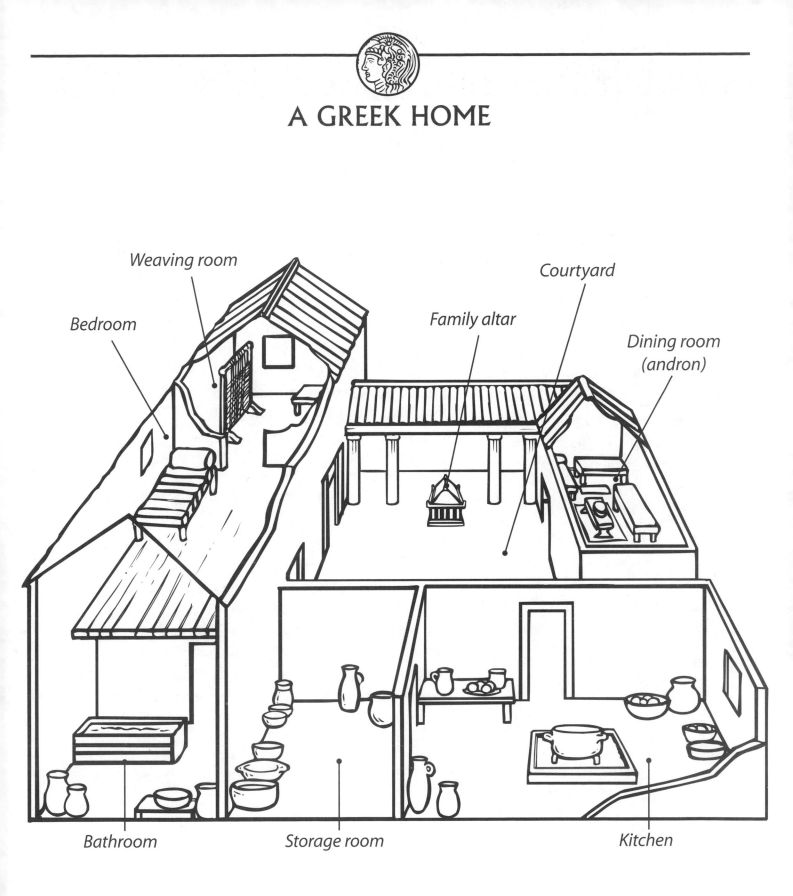

Weaving room

Bedroom

Family altar

Courtyard

Dining room
(andron)

Bathroom

Storage room

Kitchen

MOSAIC TILES

Mosaic is an art form in which small pieces of cut stone or glass are embedded in plaster.

Mosaic tiles were used by the ancient Greeks to make the floors of important rooms in their houses. The andron was the room in which men entertained their guests. Mosaic tile floors were often found there.

Students design and create their own mosaic tile "floors."

MATERIALS

- 1" (2.5 cm) squares of paper in assorted colors
- 8" x 8" (20 x 20 cm) white construction paper
- 9" x 12" (23 x 30.5 cm) colored construction paper
- writing paper, cut into a strip of 5 lines
- pencil
- scissors
- glue

STEPS TO FOLLOW

1. Discuss the art form of mosaic and the fact that it originated in ancient Greece. Share pictures of mosaics from reference books, and bring in actual mosaics if possible.

2. Pass out the white construction paper squares. Tell students that this is their plain floor tile.

3. Direct students to use the colored squares to make a mosaic pattern on the plain floor tile. Tell them to leave small, equal spaces between the colored pieces to resemble the look of mortar. Encourage them to cut the colored squares into rectangles and triangles to make a more complicated pattern.

4. After they are happy with the pattern, have them glue the mosaic pieces into place.

5. After the mosaic tile is dry, have students glue the mosaic tile to the larger piece of construction paper.

6. You may want to have them create a decorative border around the completed floor tile for added interest.

7. Write the definition of *mosaic* on the board. Direct students to copy the definition on writing paper, and then glue it to the back of the tile.

   EMC 3705 • Ancient Greece • ©2003 by Evan-Moor Corp.

A GREEK WEDDING

Ancient Greek weddings were cause for celebration just as they are today. Students read about marriage customs in ancient Greece, noting the similarities and differences between an ancient Greek wedding and a modern-day ceremony.

Students make an invitation to a wedding ceremony of Helen and Philip of Athens.

STEPS TO FOLLOW

1. Read and discuss the information about the marriage ceremony with students.

2. Tell them they are going to make a wedding invitation for two people named Helen and Philip of Athens.

3. Pass out the invitation pattern to students and guide them through the following steps:

   a. Write the necessary details for the wedding in the center square of the pattern on page 29.

   b. Decorate all four petals with pictures of items mentioned on page 28.

   c. Cut out the card and seal patterns.

   d. Fold the "flower petals" on the fold lines, closing the card.

   e. Decorate the outside of the invitation as well.

   f. Glue the paper seal onto one petal only, so that the card can be opened.

MATERIALS

- pages 28 and 29, reproduced for each student
- pencil
- marking pens
- scissors
- glue
- Optional: stickers, wrapping paper scraps, and ribbons for decorations

⊞ A GREEK MARRIAGE CEREMONY ⊞

The marriage ceremony was an important event in ancient Greece. The groom, chosen by the bride's father, might have been as old as 30. A girl usually married at the age of 14 or 15. The father of the bride provided a dowry. This was a gift of money and goods that was given to the new husband.

The day before the wedding, the bride sacrificed all her toys to the goddess Artemis to symbolize the end of her childhood. On the day of the wedding, both families made sacrifices to the gods and held feasts in separate houses. The bride dressed in her best clothes and put on a veil. The veil was crowned with a wreath of leaves.

Then, in the afternoon, the groom and his best man went to the bride's home. This was often the first time the bride and groom had met. There was another feast. After the meal, the wedding guests gave gifts to the new couple. Gifts included furniture, jewelry, mirrors, perfumes, vases, and baskets. As night came, the father of the bride gave his daughter to the groom.

Now everyone got ready for the procession from the bride's home to the groom's home. If the couple came from a wealthy family, they rode in a chariot. Poorer brides and grooms rode in carts. The guests followed the bride and groom, carrying torches and more wedding gifts. As they walked, the guests sang a marriage hymn. At the door of the groom's house, his parents met the couple. The bride was carried over the threshold as a symbol that she was joining a new family. The guests sang very loudly as they entered to ward off any evil spirits. The family and guests then scattered fruits, nuts, and flowers over the couple to bring them good health and prosperity.

Do some of these traditions sound familiar? Of course, now men and women choose who and when they are going to marry, but some of the same traditions are carried out in modern weddings.

EMC 3705 • Ancient Greece • ©2003 by Evan-Moor Corp.

▦ A WEDDING INVITATION ▦

Card

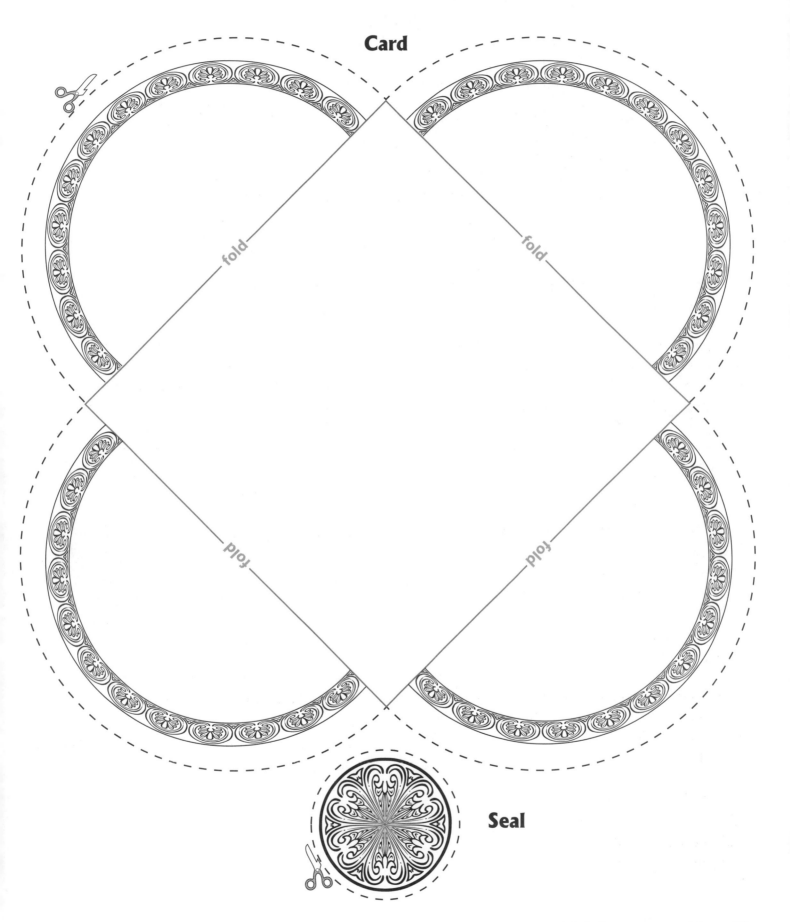

fold

fold

fold

fold

Seal

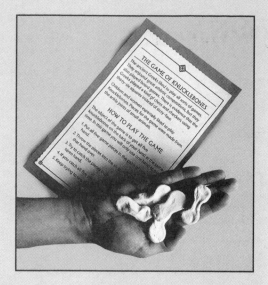

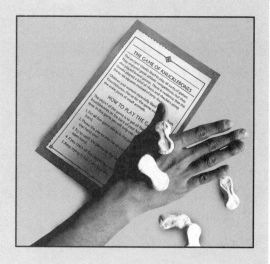

MATERIALS

- page 31, reproduced for students
- self-hardening clay
- 5" x 8" (13 x 20 cm) construction paper
- glue
- reclosable plastic bag, quart size
- Optional: paints and paintbrush

THE GAME OF KNUCKLEBONES

The game of Knucklebones was a popular game played by women and children. Small bones were thrown into the air and caught on the back of the hand. It took great skill to get all five game pieces to land on the back of the hand.

Students get a chance to make five knucklebones and then play this ancient Greek game of skill.

STEPS TO FOLLOW

1. Guide students through the following steps to make the five playing pieces for Knucklebones:

    a. Divide a ball of clay into five equal pieces.

    b. Roll each piece of clay into a small ball.

    c. Press the ball into a peanut shape that is about 1" (2.5 cm) long.

    d. Make small dents in the ends of each piece to flatten.

    e. Let the game pieces dry. Paint if desired.

2. Read the playing directions with students. Have students glue the directions onto construction paper.

3. Let students try their skill at the game. Then store the game pieces and the game rules in a reclosable plastic bag.

4. Optional: To extend the activity or to make the game more challenging, you may want to have students revise the game to include directions on how to play the game with two or more players.

THE GAME OF KNUCKLEBONES

The ancient Greeks liked to play all sorts of games. They enjoyed great athletic competitions, but they also played board games. There is evidence that the Greeks played a kind of chess and checkers, using 36 squares instead of 64.

Children and women especially liked to play Knucklebones. Pieces for the game were made from the ankle joints of small animals.

HOW TO PLAY THE GAME

The object of the game is to get all five knucklebones on the back of your hand at the same time. In this game you will only use one hand to play.

1. Place all five game pieces in the palm of one hand.

2. Throw the pieces into the air and quickly flip that hand over.

3. Try to catch the pieces on the back of your open hand.

4. If you catch all five pieces, you win.

5. Keep trying to see if you improve.

Pocket 4
GOVERNMENT

FAST FACTS

See page 2 for information on how to prepare the Fast Facts bookmark and pocket label. Use the bookmark for a quick review during transition times throughout the day.

ABOUT

Reproduce this page for students. Read about and discuss the government of ancient Greece, highlighting important information to remember. Incorporate library and multimedia resources that are available.

ART REFERENCE

Use this reproducible page as a reference for the activities in the pocket.

ACTIVITIES

Pericles was a great persuasive orator in Athens. He was able to convince the Athenians to make sweeping changes to their city-state. Students become orators when they give their own persuasive speeches to an audience.

Reproduce pages 38 and 39 for each student. Read and discuss the life and trial of the great philosopher, Socrates. Have students pretend they are Socrates' students and answer questions about the meaning of life asked on page 39. You may wish to have students glue the information to one side of a piece of construction paper and their answers to the other side.

Athenian jurors were given two ballots or tokens with which to cast a vote of guilty or not guilty. Students make their own ballots, and then use them to vote on an important classroom or school issue.

GOVERNMENT

GOVERNMENT
FAST FACTS

- There were 300 city-states in ancient Greece. Every city-state was called a polis, from which our word *politics* comes.

- Sparta was ruled by both the military and kings. This is called totalitarianism.

- In 508 B.C. Cleisthenes came into power in Athens. He set up a new kind of assembly government called democracy, which means "rule by the people."

- Athens had a population of about 315,000 people; 43,000 were considered citizens. Citizens were free men who had been born in the city-state.

- Metics were free men who had been born outside the city. Metics had to pay taxes and could serve in the army but could never become citizens or own property.

- Our word *polite* comes from the Greek tradition of needing to be quiet to hear speakers at assembly meetings where there might be 6,000 citizens present.

- Juries were always made up of an odd number so there was not an even split in the vote.

- Pericles was the most famous politician in Athens. He was a powerful orator, or public speaker. He was elected to the Council every year until his death in 429 B.C.

ABOUT
GOVERNMENT IN ATHENS

The origins of democracy and trial by jury began in Athens. Both were remarkable achievements of ancient Greece.

The word *democracy* comes from two Greek words—*demos* (people) and *kratos* (rule).

The Athenians set up an assembly where every male citizen could speak and vote. There had to be at least 6,000 citizens present for a meeting to take place. Women, slaves, and men born outside the city were all excluded from the assembly.

The assembly met every 9 or 10 days on a hill called the Pnyx and debated proposals made by the Council. Often the proposal was whether to declare war on another nation. The Council was made up of 500 citizens— 50 elected from each of the 10 tribes in Athens. The important officials were the 10 strategoi, military commanders, who were elected every year to lead the Council.

The Athenians also developed the first trial-by-jury system. It was the duty of all citizens over the age of 30 to serve on a jury. The jury usually consisted of about 201 to 2,001 citizens. A jury heard about the crime and then voted to decide whether the person on trial was innocent or guilty. Each juror had two small bronze tokens called ballots. A ballot with a solid center meant not guilty, and a ballot with a hollow center meant guilty.

If a person was found guilty, the punishment was supposed to fit the crime. Criminals could be fined or have their property taken. If someone was considered a threat to the government, they were ostracized. This meant the person had to leave Athens for 10 years. Murderers were executed immediately. The only people that were put in prison were foreigners or criminals awaiting execution.

EMC 3705 • Ancient Greece • ©2003 by Evan-Moor Corp.

GOVERNMENT IN ATHENS

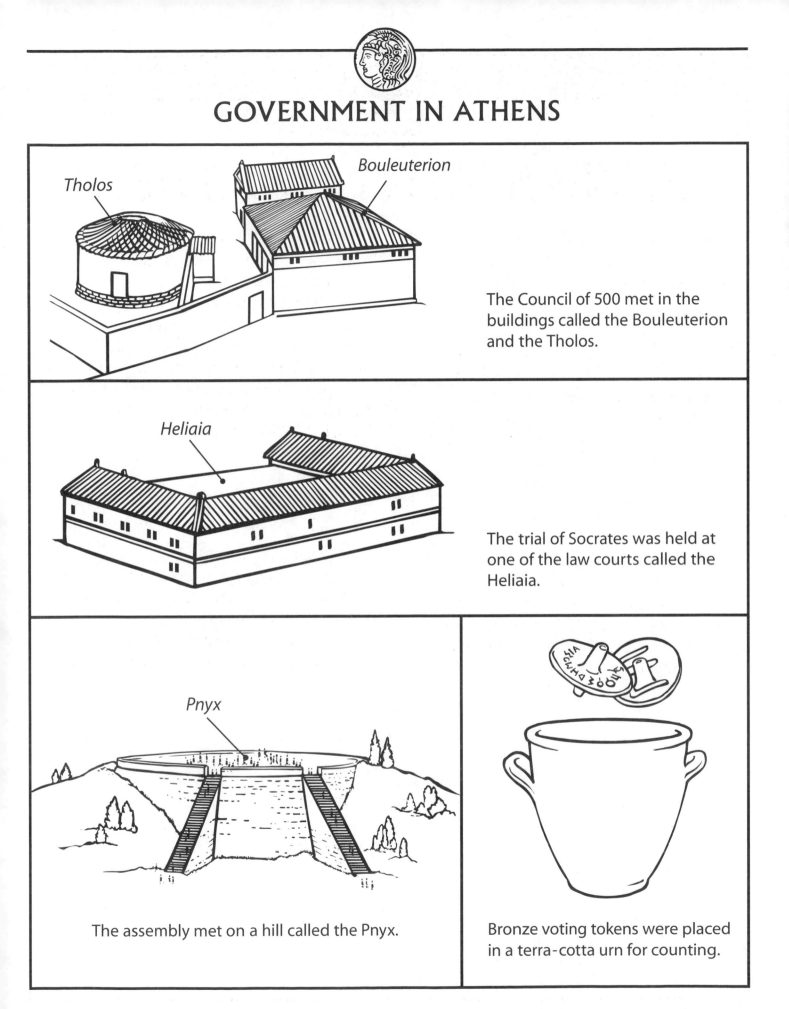

Tholos

Bouleuterion

The Council of 500 met in the buildings called the Bouleuterion and the Tholos.

Heliaia

The trial of Socrates was held at one of the law courts called the Heliaia.

Pnyx

The assembly met on a hill called the Pnyx.

Bronze voting tokens were placed in a terra-cotta urn for counting.

MATERIALS

- page 37, reproduced for each student
- 9" x 12" (23 x 30.5 cm) black construction paper
- pencil
- scissors
- glue

THE ART OF PERSUASION

The Greeks loved rhetoric, which was the art of speaking and writing persuasively. In a persuasive speech, the speaker has a strong opinion to express and tries to get the audience to believe or act as the speaker wants. It is important that the speaker be seen as intelligent and trustworthy. The speaker must also relate to the audience on a personal level.

Pericles, a leader of Athens, was considered one of the finest orators, or speakers, of ancient Greece. He was able to convince the people of Athens to build expensive, new public buildings and temples. He convinced them to build a more powerful navy. He demanded that power be spread more evenly between the rich and the poor.

Students become great orators when they write and give persuasive speeches on a chosen topic.

STEPS TO FOLLOW

1. Discuss the information about persuasive speeches with students.

2. As a class, brainstorm possible topics for the students to use for their speeches. Possible issues may include such things as increasing the school day or year, cutting fine arts programs in the school, or wearing school uniforms.

3. As the teacher, decide if you are going to allow a choice of topics or have all students write and give speeches on the same topic.

4. Have students use the temple form on page 37 to write a short speech (around two minutes).

5. Direct students to cut out and glue the speech form to black construction paper, and then trim around it to create a border.

6. Encourage students to practice their speeches and go over the "Tips for a Good Speech."

7. Allow time in class for students to give their speeches to an audience.

EMC 3705 • Ancient Greece • ©2003 by Evan-Moor Corp.

⊞ THE ART OF PERSUASION ⊞

Topic

Tips for a Good Speech
• Speak loudly and clearly • Speak slowly • Look at your audience • Use good posture • Show enthusiasm

Introduction

Get the audience's attention with a powerful beginning.

Body

Explain the need or problem. Explain your idea that answers the need or problem. Give facts and examples to support your idea.

Conclusion

Ask the audience to take action.

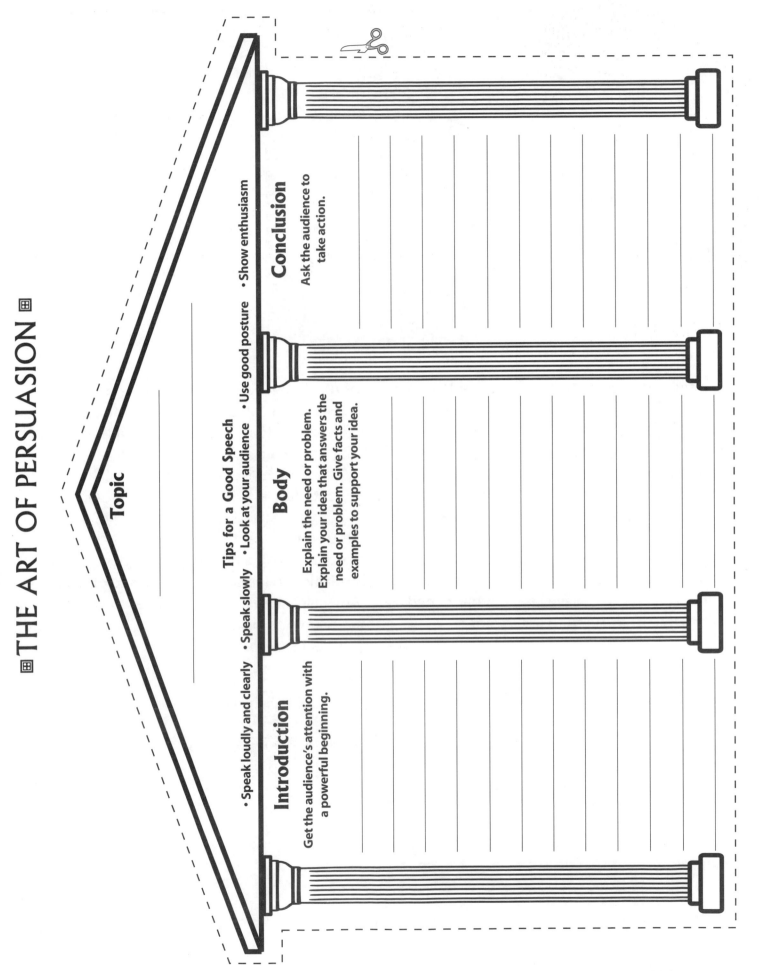

• EMC 3705 • Ancient Greece

⊞ SOCRATES, A GREAT TEACHER ⊞

Socrates was a famous philosopher and teacher in ancient Greece. A philosopher is a person who searches for the truth about life. Socrates questioned every aspect of life. He especially liked debating the issues of good and evil. Socrates believed that no one deliberately does evil things. Socrates taught his students to think for themselves and to question everything. His teaching style was to ask questions of his students that made them examine their own beliefs. He did not believe learning happened if teachers just lectured to their students.

His method of teaching made the Athenian leaders angry. They were worried that by teaching young people to question every aspect of life, Socrates and his pupils were challenging the authority of the government. In truth, Socrates and his followers did point out weaknesses in the government and did challenge the idea of worshipping many gods.

Socrates was charged with corrupting the minds of the young and showing disrespect for the gods. Socrates stood trial in 399 B.C. at the age

of 70. He pleaded his own case before a jury of 700 Athenian citizens. The jury convicted him by a narrow margin. Socrates was given a choice for his punishment. He could leave Athens forever, or he could drink a cup of poisonous hemlock tea and die. He refused to leave his beloved Athens and chose the hemlock. Plato, one of his students, wanted to bribe the guards to let Socrates escape, but Socrates said no. Socrates explained to his friends that he had obeyed the Athenian laws all his life, and he would not break them now. Socrates drank the tea and died, with his friends surrounding him.

Socrates did not write down his original ideas, but thankfully his followers did. Socrates was considered a wise man, and the Socratic method of questioning ideas and opinions is still practiced today.

▣ SOCRATES, A GREAT TEACHER ▣

Now that you have read about Socrates, it is your turn to be one of his students. Pretend your teacher, Socrates, wants you to answer the following questions. Answer them honestly and fully. Remember, Socrates would want you to give reasons for your answers.

1. My most famous quote was, "The unexamined life is not worth living." What did I mean by this?

_____

_____

2. What makes people happy? _____

_____

_____

3. What would life be like if everyone were the same? _____

_____

_____

4. Why do we have rules in our world?_____

_____

_____

5. Do you think all people are basically good?_____

_____

_____

Now that you have answered some of Socrates' questions, you are ready to read and share your answers with a partner. Compare your answers. Remember, Socrates would value both opinions because he did not believe that any answer to a question was wrong if it was a well-thought-out idea.

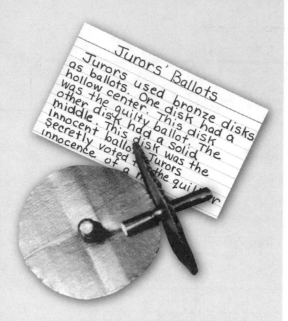

MATERIALS

- corrugated cardboard
- scissors
- hole punch
- drinking straw
- small wooden dowel pin (packages found at hardware stores)
- bronze-colored paint
- paintbrush
- bowl of water
- newspaper
- black marking pen
- 3" x 5" (7.5 x 13 cm) index card
- plastic storage bag

JURORS' BALLOTS

During a trial in Athens, there were as many as 2,001 jurors who decided if the person was guilty or not guilty. Jurors were given two bronze disks to be used as ballots. The center of one of the disks was hollow. This disk meant the juror thought the accused was guilty. The middle of the other disk was solid. This disk indicated that the juror thought the accused was not guilty. The jurors placed the ballots in an urn to be counted secretly. The verdict was then read, and the court gave the sentence.

Students make their own ballots to use to vote on a classroom issue.

STEPS TO FOLLOW

1. Discuss with students the two kinds of ballots jurors used in trials.

2. Tell students that they are going to make two ballots and then vote on an important issue in class.

3. Have students follow these directions to make their ballots:

   a. Cut two 2" (5 cm) circles from corrugated cardboard.

   b. Punch a hole in each circle.

   c. Cut the drinking straw into fourths. Place one of the pieces of the drinking straw into the hole of one of the circles. This is the "guilty" ballot.

   d. Place a wooden dowel in the other circle. This is the "not guilty" ballot.

   e. Paint both circles using bronze-colored paint. Allow them to dry.

   f. Using a marking pen, students write their initials or names on the ballots.

4. Instruct students to use the index card to write a short paragraph about the two ballots and how they were used in ancient Greek trials.

5. As a class, have students vote on a school or classroom issue using the ballots. Collect the secret ballots in an "urn" to be counted. Make the announcement in class, and then return the ballots to the students.

6. Have students store the ballots and the index card in the storage bag.

EMC 3705 • Ancient Greece • ©2003 by Evan-Moor Corp.

Pocket 5
RELIGION AND MYTHOLOGY

FAST FACTS

See page 2 for information on how to prepare the Fast Facts bookmark and pocket label. Use the bookmark for a quick review during transition times throughout the day.

ABOUT

Reproduce this page for students. Read about and discuss the religion and mythology of ancient Greece, highlighting important information to remember. Incorporate library and multimedia resources that are available.

ART REFERENCE

Use these reproducible pages as references for the activities in the pocket.

ACTIVITIES

Ancient Greeks prayed to many gods. The Olympian gods were the most powerful. Students learn about these gods when they make an accordion book.

The ancient Greek myths are the most famous in the world. Students read a short version of "Persephone and the Underworld" to understand the elements of a good myth. Groups then make cards naming myth story elements. Students then draw a set of element cards and write their own Greek myths. They add a picture to enhance the story.

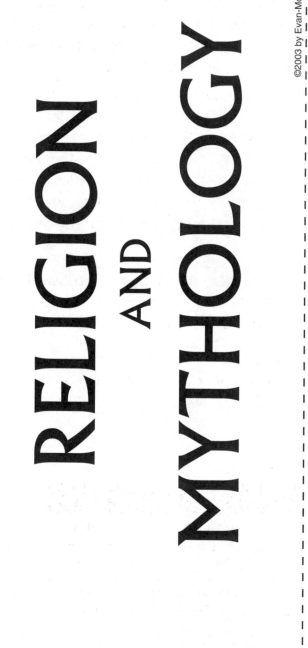

RELIGION AND MYTHOLOGY

©2003 by Evan-Moor Corp. • EMC 3705

RELIGION AND MYTHOLOGY

FAST FACTS

- The major gods were called the Olympians. People believed Zeus and his family of gods lived high above the clouds on Mount Olympus. No humans could visit Olympus unless they received a special invitation.

- Myths were an important part of Greek religion. Myths were stories about gods and heroes who could be both mortal (human) and immortal (god-like).

- For major decisions in their lives, the ancient Greeks sought the advice of the gods. They consulted an oracle, which was a priestess who spoke for a god.

- Each of the gods had a symbol that represented them in some way. Zeus, king of the gods, had a thunderbolt as his symbol. Athena's symbol was an owl, and Apollo's symbol was the lyre.

- Ancient Greeks did not want to anger the gods. They believed if Zeus got angry, he would punish them by throwing thunderbolts at the people.

- People believed that when they died, their souls were taken to the Underworld, which was ruled by the god Hades.

©2003 by Evan-Moor Corp. • EMC 3705

THE OLYMPIAN GODS ⊞

ZEUS

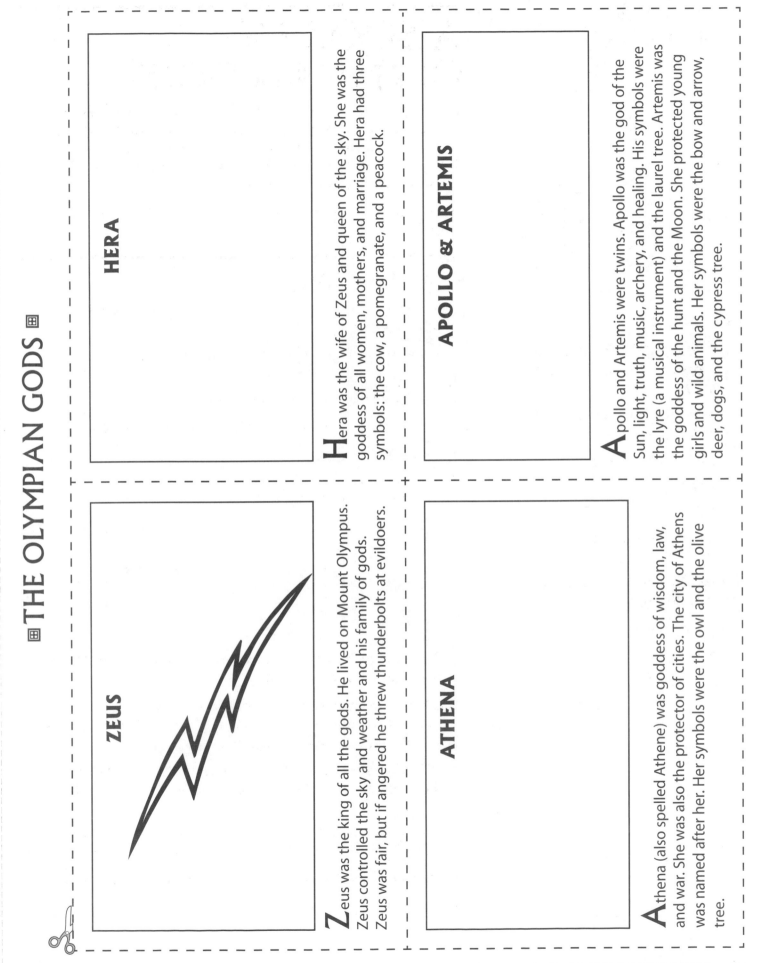

Zeus was the king of all the gods. He lived on Mount Olympus. Zeus controlled the sky and weather and his family of gods. Zeus was fair, but if angered he threw thunderbolts at evildoers.

HERA

Hera was the wife of Zeus and queen of the sky. She was the goddess of all women, mothers, and marriage. Hera had three symbols: the cow, a pomegranate, and a peacock.

ATHENA

Athena (also spelled Athene) was goddess of wisdom, law, and war. She was also the protector of cities. The city of Athens was named after her. Her symbols were the owl and the olive tree.

APOLLO & ARTEMIS

Apollo and Artemis were twins. Apollo was the god of the Sun, light, truth, music, archery, and healing. His symbols were the lyre (a musical instrument) and the laurel tree. Artemis was the goddess of the hunt and the Moon. She protected young girls and wild animals. Her symbols were the bow and arrow, deer, dogs, and the cypress tree.

▦ THE OLYMPIAN GODS ▦

APHRODITE

Aphrodite was the goddess of love and beauty. She inspired love and protected people that were in love. Her symbols were doves, roses, sparrows, dolphins, and rams.

HADES

Hades was the god of the dead and the Underworld. He was a dark and gloomy god. Hades carried a scepter and was protected by his dogs.

HERMES

Hermes was the messenger of the gods. He reported events on Earth to the gods. Hermes wore a winged hat and winged shoes, and carried a staff.

POSEIDON

Poseidon was the god of the sea and all water. He controlled storms, sea monsters, and earthquakes. Poseidon could protect or destroy ships. His symbols were a trident, dolphins, and horses.

EMC 3705 • Ancient Greece • © by Evan-Moor Corp.

THE OLYMPIAN GODS

DEMETER

Demeter was the goddess of the earth, plants, and harvests. She protected the crops in the fields. Her daughter, Persephone, helped Demeter. Her symbol was a sheaf of wheat or barley.

HEPHAESTUS

Hephaestus was the god of fire and armor. He protected craftsmen and metalsmiths while they worked on bronze weapons and tools. His symbols were a hammer and an anvil.

HESTIA

Hestia was the goddess of the hearth and home. She protected people's homes from evil. Every family had a shrine dedicated to her. She is often shown sitting in front of a wood fire.

ARES

Ares was the god of war. He was brave, angry, and terrible. Ares protected the soldiers on the fields. His symbols were a burning torch, a spear, dogs, and vultures.

MIXED-UP MYTHS

Myths are traditional stories about the lives of the gods and legendary heroes. The myths of ancient Greece are among the most famous in the world. Ancient Greeks lacked today's scientific knowledge, so myths were often created to explain the mysteries of nature. Besides gods and heroes, the myths also contained monsters, magic, and amazing adventures.

Students read and enjoy a well-known Greek myth to understand the story elements of myths. Then they write their own original myths.

STEPS TO FOLLOW

1. Explain the definition of a myth to students.

2. Hand out page 51 and read a short version of a myth. Read other Greek myths from your library, if available.

3. Hand out page 52 and discuss with students the story elements: characters, setting, problem or situation, and ending or resolution. Remind students that often a myth explained something in nature or gave a lesson to be learned.

4. Divide students into groups of four and pass out index cards.

5. Direct each group to write the story elements from page 52 on cards.

    a. Write the 12 characters, one per card.

    b. Write the 6 settings, one per card.

    c. Write the 6 problems, one per card.

    d. Write the 6 endings, one per card.

6. Instruct students to put the character, setting, problem, and ending cards, each in separate piles facedown on the table.

7. Without looking at the cards, each student in the group draws two character cards, one setting card, one problem card, and one ending card.

8. Instruct students go back to their desks and use these five cards to write their own version of a myth on the writing form on page 53. (Some students may need additional paper.)

9. Have students mount their myths on construction paper. They illustrate the myth and glue the picture on the back.

10. Encourage students to share their myths with their groups.

MATERIALS

- pages 51 and 53, reproduced for each student
- page 52, reproduced for each group of four students
- 30 small index cards per group of four students
- 9" x 12" (23 x 30.5 cm) colored construction paper
- pencil
- glue
- crayons or colored pencils
- books containing Greek myths

⊞ MIXED-UP MYTHS ⊞
PERSEPHONE AND THE GOD OF THE UNDERWORLD

Persephone was the lovely daughter of Demeter, goddess of the harvest. One day Persephone wandered off while helping her mother in the garden. Hades, god of the Underworld, saw Persephone and immediately fell in love with her. Hades grabbed poor Persephone and swept her off to his gloomy underground palace.

Hades made her a beautiful throne and gave her precious jewels and fine robes. This did not please Persephone, who missed the sunlight of Earth and her mother. She refused to eat the food of the dead that Hades gave her. Only a few seeds from a pomegranate kept her alive.

On the earth above, Demeter was beside herself with grief over the loss of her daughter. She was so depressed and angry that she refused to let anything grow. The earth became icy and the plants died. People and animals were starving, and the gods pleaded with Demeter to bless the earth again.

Zeus knew he must help the earth, even though he hesitated to interfere with Hades' plans. After all, Hades was his brother. Zeus called Hermes, messenger of the gods, to tell Hades that he must release Persephone for at least part of the year.

On winged feet, Hermes sped downward to the Underworld. He told Hades that Zeus had ordered the release of Persephone. Persephone would stay with Hades half of the year, but she would get to live with her mother on Earth the other half. Hades dared not disobey the king of the gods, so he sent Persephone home in a chariot.

Demeter was so happy to see her daughter that she blessed the earth and it blossomed anew again.

STORY ELEMENTS

Characters: Persephone, Demeter, Hades, Zeus, and Hermes

Setting: Earth and the Underworld

Problem or situation: The earth died when Demeter was sad.

Ending or resolution: The earth came alive when Persephone returned to her mother.

Explanation: This Greek myth explains the changing of the seasons from winter to spring.

⊞ MIXED-UP MYTHS ⊞
STORY ELEMENTS OF A MYTH

CHARACTERS

Zeus, king of the gods

Hera, queen of the gods

Athena, goddess of wisdom and war

Apollo, god of the Sun, light, and music

Artemis, goddess of the hunt

Hermes, messenger of the gods

Aphrodite, goddess of love and beauty

Poseidon, god of the sea

Hestia, goddess of the home and hearth

Demeter, goddess of the harvest

Ares, god of war

Hades, god of the Underworld

(other gods and heroes may be added to your list)

SETTINGS

agora, a busy marketplace

Acropolis, sacred hill

Mount Olympus, home of the gods

Olympic Games, at Olympia

Parthenon, temple for Athena

Aegean Sea

(other places may be added to your list)

PROBLEMS OR SITUATIONS

earthquake shakes city

monsters in the sea

solar eclipse

volcanic eruption

battle for power

love and jealousy

(other problems may be added to your list)

ENDINGS OR RESOLUTIONS

built a new temple

reclaimed the kingdom

sent to Sparta to live

defeated the serpent

rode off on a golden chariot

found the treasure

(other endings may be added to your list)

EMC 3705 • Ancient Greece • ©2003 by Evan-Moor Corp.

Name: _____

▣ MY VERY OWN MIXED-UP MYTH ▣

Write the elements on your cards below.

CHARACTERS	SETTING
_____ _____	_____ _____
PROBLEM OR SITUATION	**ENDING OR RESOLUTION**
_____ _____	_____ _____

_____
title

_____
_____
_____
_____
_____
_____
_____
_____
_____
_____
_____

Pocket 6
WORK AND SCHOOL

FAST FACTS

See page 2 for information on how to prepare the Fast Facts bookmark and pocket label. Use the bookmark for a quick review during transition times throughout the day.

ABOUT

Reproduce this page for students. Read about and discuss work and school in ancient Greece, highlighting important information to remember. Incorporate library and multimedia resources that are available.

ART REFERENCE

Use this reproducible page as a reference for the activities in the pocket.

ACTIVITIES

The agora was a busy marketplace filled with all kinds of shops and vendor stalls. After reading page 58, students decide what kind of business to run at the agora. They follow the directions to make a sign advertising their shop. Provide 9" x 12" (23 x 30.5 cm) light-colored construction paper and a variety of craft supplies and marking pens to make the sign.

Sparta was the only city-state that did not use coins for money. They used iron bars. Students help out Sparta by creating a coin the Spartans would have liked.

There were many great thinkers in ancient Greece who helped define the schools of science and mathematics. Students choose a school they would like to attend in ancient Greece, and then give reasons for their decision.

WORK AND SCHOOL

(vertical title, left panel)

WORK AND SCHOOL
FAST FACTS

- Coins were first used in ancient Greece. The earliest coins were small lumps of electrum, which is a mixture of gold and silver. Later, coins were solid gold or silver.

- Money-changers helped people find ways to invest their coins and then paid them interest from the profits.

- Attica, the region around Athens, was famous for its olive trees. Olive oil was used for cooking and washing. Olive oil was also used in cosmetics, lamps, and medicines.

- Metalsmiths worked in small workshops at home. They used bronze, iron, silver, and gold to make their wares. Metalsmiths were so admired that they had their own god, Hephaestus, to look after them.

- Athenian boys of wealthy families attended schools. Slaves called Paidotribes helped the boys with their homework and made sure the boys behaved for the teachers.

- The idea of a higher education began in ancient Greece. Sophists went from city to city instructing young men in the art of public speaking.

- The great philosopher Aristotle tutored Alexander the Great when he was young.

- Hippocrates, called the father of medicine, founded a medical school. He had his students take an oath to use their medical skills to heal and never to harm. Doctors still say the Hippocratic oath today.

ABOUT
WORK AND SCHOOL

Farmers, fishermen, and craftspeople were all important to the economy of ancient Greece.

Even though the soil was rocky and poor, most ancient Greeks worked the land. Farmers grew barley, a staple in the Greek diet. The hilly land was well-suited for growing olives and grapes.

Farmers and fishermen brought their products to the marketplace. The agora, the marketplace in Athens, was a large open square located near the Acropolis. It was crowded with food stalls, shops, and workshops. Craftsmen such as stone carvers and metalworkers sold their products at the agora. Inspectors made sure that shopkeepers were not cheating their customers. They carried standard weights and measures to weigh the products and the coins.

The ancient Greeks used coins for their money beginning in 690 B.C. Each city-state made its own silver coins. The city name and representative picture was stamped on each coin. Up to 20,000 slaves worked in the mines to produce the silver for the coins.

Slaves were a vital part of the workforce for ancient Greece. Wealthy families used 50 or more slaves. Even poor farmers used slaves to help with the work. Slaves were brought to Greece from as far away as Eastern Europe and Asia. Because slaves did most of the work, middle-class and wealthy boys and men could devote more time toward school and developing new ideas and inventions.

Boys in Athens learned from the great thinkers of the day. Besides the basics, students learned philosophy, history, poetry, and music. They were also expected to train for competitive sports and military service. Being a soldier was the greatest job a Greek man could have.

Ancient Greece produced some of the greatest thinkers the world has ever known. Archimedes invented the principle of the useful lever. Hipparchus invented trigonometry. Euclid is called the father of geometry, and Pythagoras is noted for his rules of geometry. Hippocrates was the founder of modern medicine.

EMC 3705 • Ancient Greece • ©2003 by Evan-Moor Corp.

THE AGORA

⊞ WORKING AT THE AGORA ⊞

The agora was a busy marketplace. Originally, farmers came to small marketplaces to trade their goods. Then when coins were introduced around 690 B.C., city-states like Athens built large central marketplaces.

Open-air tented stalls, where people could buy cooked food and drink, lined the marketplace. Craftsmen set up tables to sell their goods. Money-changers also sat at tables to help people invest their extra coins. You could hear the shopkeepers beckoning their customers to come over to their stalls. Local farmers sold their products right off their donkeys and horses.

In the middle of the open-air agora was a round platform called a kykloi. People stood on this platform to speak about the politics of the day. It was also used to sell slaves. Most agoras also had an altar or statue honoring a local god and a large fountain where people came to drink and visit.

Families could be seen strolling in the agora. It was rare to see women alone in public because they always had to be accompanied by male relatives. Men did the shopping for the family. The agora was a bustling place in ancient Greece.

DIRECTIONS

Pretend you are an ancient Greek who wants to open a new business at the agora. Choose a business that interests you the most. You might sell a craft or food item, perhaps something you grew.

Fold a piece of construction paper in half lengthwise to form a stand-up sign to sit on a table. On the front of the sign, write the name of your shop and what kinds of things you are selling. Use art supplies to decorate the sign to attract buyers to your shop.

On the back of the sign, write a "sales pitch" that will make people want to buy your product.

SCHOOLS OF THOUGHT

The ancient Greeks devoted much time to studying and thinking. A new scientific way of thinking developed in Greece, based on theory and practice rather than on old superstitions. Many great scientists made discoveries in mathematics and medicine.

Students traveled long distances to learn from the great thinkers at academies and colleges. Pythagoras set up a community of mathematical scholars who studied geometric theorems. Euclid, a mathematician, wrote a geometry textbook called *Elements*, which was used for over 2,000 years.

Hippocrates, called the father of medicine, ran a training school for doctors. His students were asked to swear a solemn oath to live pure and holy lives and to use their medical skills to heal and never to harm. Doctors today recite the Hippocratic oath when they graduate from medical school.

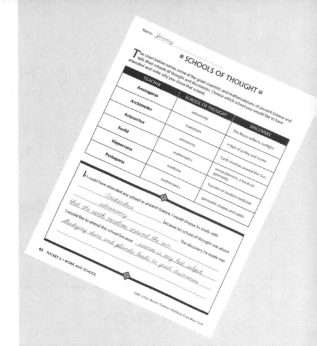

STEPS TO FOLLOW

1. Share with students the information above about the great thinkers of ancient Greece. You may wish to reproduce the information on an overhead transparency.

2. Read the chart on page 62 with students, and then instruct them to choose a teacher and a school of thought.

3. Students complete the form on page 62, telling why they chose that particular school of thought.

MATERIALS

- page 62, reproduced for each student
- pencil

Name: _____

▣ SCHOOLS OF THOUGHT ▣

The chart below names some of the great scientists and mathematicians of ancient Greece and tells their schools of thought and discoveries. Choose which school you would like to have attended and write why you chose that school.

TEACHER	SCHOOL OF THOUGHT	DISCOVERY
Anaxagoras	astronomy	The Moon reflects sunlight.
Archimedes	inventions	a type of lever and screw
Aristarchus	astronomy	Earth revolves around the Sun.
Euclid	mathematics	wrote *Elements,* a book on geometry
Hippocrates	medicine	founder of modern medicine
Pythagoras	mathematics	geometric shapes and solids

If I could have attended any school in ancient Greece, I would choose to study with

_____ because his school of thought was about

_____ . The discovery he made was

_____ .

I would like to attend this school because _____

_____

_____ .

     EMC 3705 • Ancient Greece • ©2003 by Evan-Moor Corp.

Pocket 7
ART AND ARCHITECTURE

FAST FACTS

Art and Architecture . . . . **page 64**
See page 2 for information on how to prepare the Fast Facts bookmark and pocket label. Use the bookmark for a quick review during transition times throughout the day.

ABOUT

Art and Architecture . . . . **page 65**
Reproduce this page for students. Read about and discuss the art and architecture of ancient Greece, highlighting important information to remember. Incorporate library and multimedia resources that are available.

ART REFERENCE

Greek Architecture; Greek Art . . . . **pages 66 & 67**
Use these reproducible pages as references for the activities in the pocket.

ACTIVITIES

The Parthenon . . . . **pages 68–70**
Students make a pop-up model of the Parthenon, and then write a paragraph describing one of the most beautiful and famous buildings in the world.

Classic Columns . . . . **page 71**
Look around and you can see examples of the classic Greek columns in many public buildings. Students use the Doric, Ionic, or Corinthian style of columns to design a new public library for their city.

An Amazing Amphora . . . . **pages 72 & 73**
The amphora was a huge jar used to store wine, water, and olive oil. Students use their geometry skills when they draw and color a perfectly symmetrical amphora jar.

Fresco of the Sea . . . . **page 74**
Students re-create a Minoan queen's beautiful fresco of dolphins and fish.

ART AND ARCHITECTURE

ART AND ARCHITECTURE

FAST FACTS

- The Parthenon, the temple dedicated to the goddess Athena, was built beginning in 446 B.C. It took 15 years to complete.

- To build the Parthenon, workers transported 22,000 tons (21,652 metric tonnes) of marble over 9 miles (15 km).

- Inside the Parthenon was a large statue of Athena made of wood and ivory. Her golden robes were removed whenever there was fear of the city being attacked. The statue cost more to make than the Parthenon itself.

- The Parthenon can still be seen today in Greece. It survived almost intact for over 2,000 years before an explosion caused the center of the temple to be blown out.

- Many of the sculptures from the Parthenon were brought to England. They are called the *Elgin Marbles* and can be seen in the British Museum.

- Friezes were carved marble decorations that appeared on all four sides of Greek temples. They commonly showed the figures of gods or heroes.

- The amphora was the most famous design in Greek pottery. It is a two-handled jar used to store wine, water, or olive oil.

ABOUT
ART AND ARCHITECTURE

In Greek history, the years 500 to 323 B.C. are called the Classical period, or the Golden Age of Athens. During this time, Athens became the dominant city-state. The Athenian leader Pericles was determined to make Athens the most beautiful city in the world. He ordered the construction of new public buildings and temples filled with magnificent sculptures and paintings.

Pericles set out to rebuild the temples on the Acropolis that were in ruins. The Acropolis was a hill high above Athens. Only sacred temples and shrines could be built there. The largest temple on the Acropolis was the Parthenon, which was made of white marble. It stood 60 feet (18 m) tall. The temple was surrounded by 46 Doric columns, each 43 feet (13 m) tall. A frieze of brightly painted carvings showed scenes from Athena's life. Inside the temple stood a 40-foot (12 m) statue of Athena.

Large columns held up the heavy stone roofs of Greek buildings. Each column had grooves, called fluting, running up and down. The top of a Greek column, called the capital, came in three different styles. The Doric capital was the simplest style.

The Ionic capital was thinner and was decorated with a scroll-like design. The Corinthian capital was elaborate and decorated with leaves.

Greek architectural style has remained popular for over 2,000 years. You can see it in many public buildings in Europe and North America, such as the U.S. Capitol Building in Washington, D.C.

Greek temples, public buildings, and homes of the wealthy were filled with beautiful paintings and pottery. Frescos were large wall paintings made by applying paint to wet plaster. The scenes on the colorful frescos were very fanciful.

Ancient Greek pottery was useful as well as beautiful. Pots were used as containers for wine, water, and olive oil. Two techniques were used to decorate pottery. In the black-figure method, black figures were painted onto natural red clay. In the red-figure method, the figures were etched directly into the red clay. The background was then filled with a solution that turned black when the pots were fired in a kiln.

GREEK ARCHITECTURE

Temple

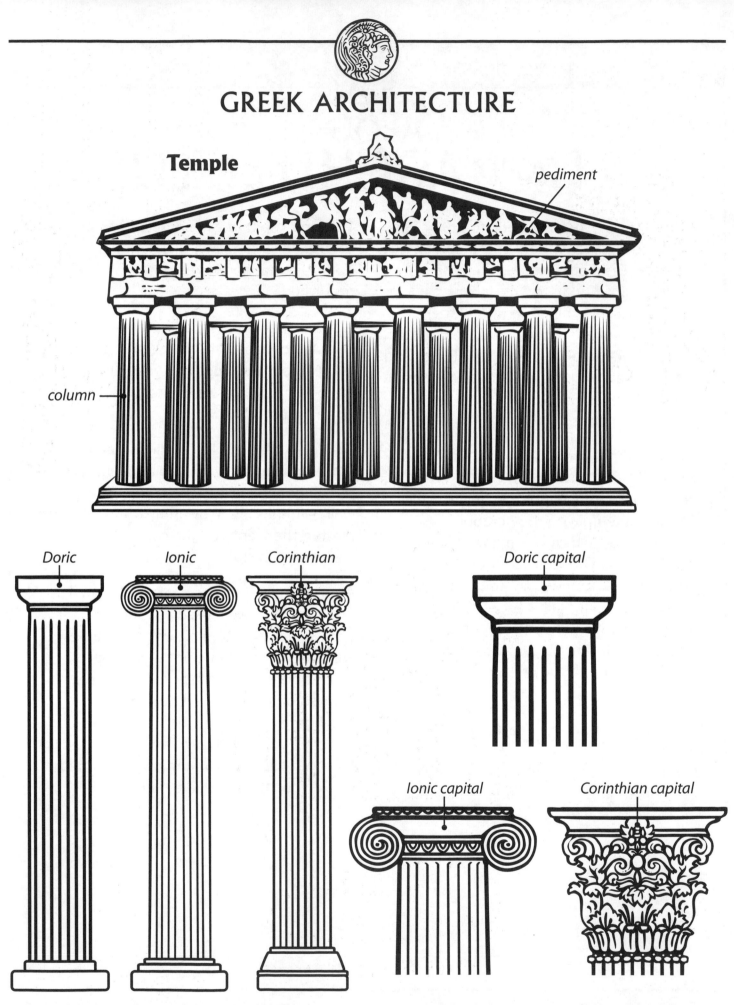

pediment

column

Doric

Ionic

Corinthian

Doric capital

Ionic capital

Corinthian capital

GREEK ART

Fresco of Bull Leapers
The Palace of Knossos, in Crete, Greece

Black-figure amphora

THE PARTHENON

The Parthenon is one of the most famous buildings in the world. Although it lies in ruins today, it was once a massive temple dedicated to the goddess Athena.

Students make a pop-up model of the Parthenon, and then write facts about the famous temple.

MATERIALS

- page 69, reproduced for each student, and page 70, reproduced for each pair of students
- 9" x 12" (23 x 30.5 cm) construction paper
- pencil
- crayons, colored pencils, or marking pens
- scissors
- glue

STEPS TO FOLLOW

1. Review the information about the Parthenon from this pocket and other resources that are available. Tell students they are going to make a pop-up model of the Parthenon.

2. Instruct students to use the writing lines on page 69 to write a paragraph of facts about the Parthenon. Remind them to look back through this pocket for information about the Parthenon.

3. Guide students through the following steps to create the pop-up:

   a. Cut out the pattern for the pop-up on page 69.

   b. Fold the card in half and cut the tab as shown.

   3b.

   c. Fold and crease the tab in both directions.

   d. Open the card and pull the tab forward.

   3c.

4. Direct students to color and cut out the Parthenon pattern.

5. Have students glue the Parthenon to the tab on the pop-up.

6. Fold the construction paper in half. Glue the pop-up inside as shown.

   Place glue on the pop-up, close the folder, and press firmly. Flip the book over and follow the same steps in gluing the back.

7. For more advanced study, you may want the students to design the statue of Athena to stand behind the Parthenon.

THE
PARTHENON

fold

fold —————————————————————————— fold

fold

◆

_____

_____

_____

_____

_____

_____

_____

THE PARTHENON

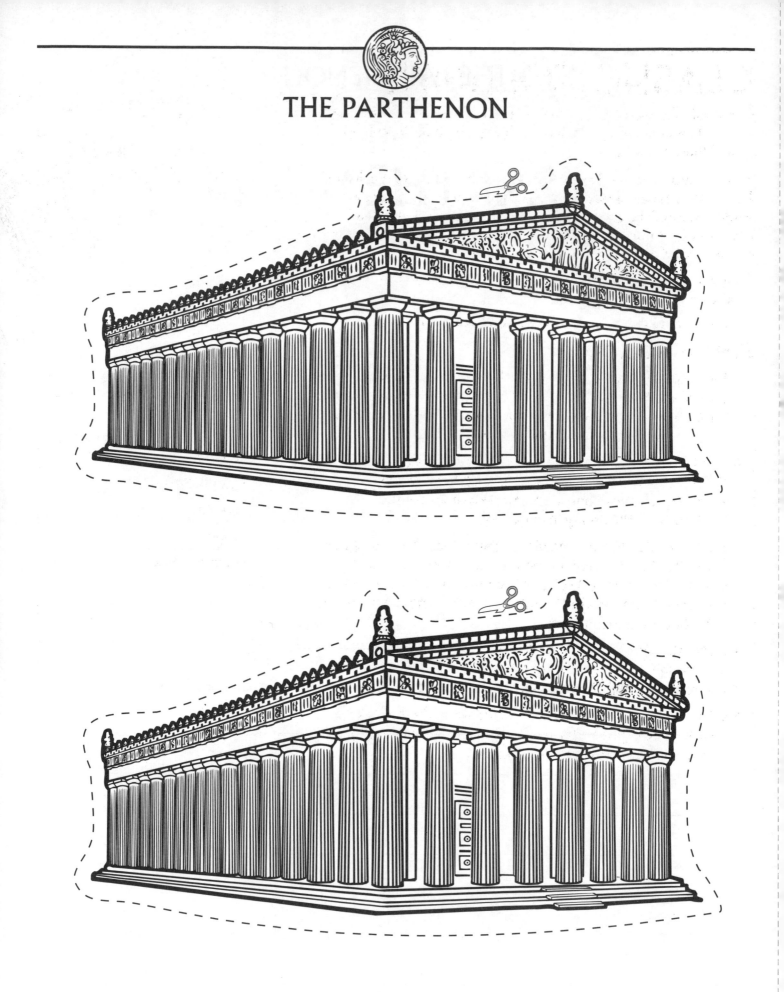

   EMC 3705 • Ancient Greece • ©2003 by Evan-Moor Corp.

CLASSIC COLUMNS

Greek columns were constructed by stacking one piece of stone at a time. The stones were so carefully fit together that the column looked like one piece.

The Romans were the first to copy the styles of the Greek columns. Examples of classic Greek columns can be seen throughout the world. Many of the government buildings in Washington, D.C., have Greek architectural style. The White House has Ionic columns, and the U.S. Capitol has Corinthian columns.

Students design a new library for their city using the Greek style of architecture.

STEPS TO FOLLOW

1. Read and discuss the use of Doric, Ionic, and Corinthian columns as described in this pocket. Have students look through reference books on ancient Greece and Washington, D.C., to see examples of Greek architecture.

2. Pass out page 66 and study the three kinds of columns and the example of a Greek temple. Tell students that they are going to choose one of the three column styles to use to design a public library for their city.

3. Instruct students to use drawing paper to make their design. Encourage students to incorporate 3 to 5 columns. Students should practice using a ruler and graph paper first to make sure the columns are the same height and width before making the final copy on drawing paper.

4. Direct students to complete the design by adding details in color. Inform them that the designs on the pediment were painted in red and blue, with gold and green accents.

5. Optional: Before students store the designs in their pockets, display the designs and have a "committee" decide which design will be used for the new library.

MATERIALS

- page 66, reproduced for each student
- 9" x 12" (23 x 30.5 cm) white drawing paper
- graph paper
- pencil
- ruler
- colored pencils

AN AMAZING AMPHORA

Skilled craftsmen of ancient Greece made beautiful pottery that became an important export. Craftsmen made pottery vases of different shapes according to their different uses. The most recognizable vase was the amphora, a two-handled jar with a flared neck. Amphorae were used to store and transport wine, water, or olive oil. They held about 10 gallons (38 L).

Students use their geometry skills when they complete the symmetrical picture of the amphora jar.

MATERIALS

- page 73, reproduced for each student
- 9" x 12" (23 x 30.5 cm) colored construction paper
- scratch paper
- pencil
- fine-tipped marking pens or colored pencils
- scissors
- glue
- writing paper
- pictures of Grecian pottery

STEPS TO FOLLOW

1. Discuss Grecian pottery and the amphora, using the information found in this pocket. Show pictures of Grecian pottery using resources that are available. (An Internet search for Greek pottery will supply a number of sites with drawings and photographs.)

2. Pass out page 73 and talk about symmetry (the exact matching of shapes on opposite sides of dividing lines).

3. Instruct students to draw the other side of the amphora, making it as symmetrical as they can. You may want to have extra copies available for students who have difficulty with this task.

4. Have students make designs on the jar and then color it. They may wish to use the black-figure technique or the red-figure technique as described on page 65.

5. Instruct students to cut out the amphora and mount it on construction paper.

6. Students use the information they have learned about the amphora to write a descriptive paragraph. Glue the paragraph to the back of the picture.

EMC 3705 • Ancient Greece • ©2003 by Evan-Moor Corp.

⊞ AN AMAZING AMPHORA ⊞

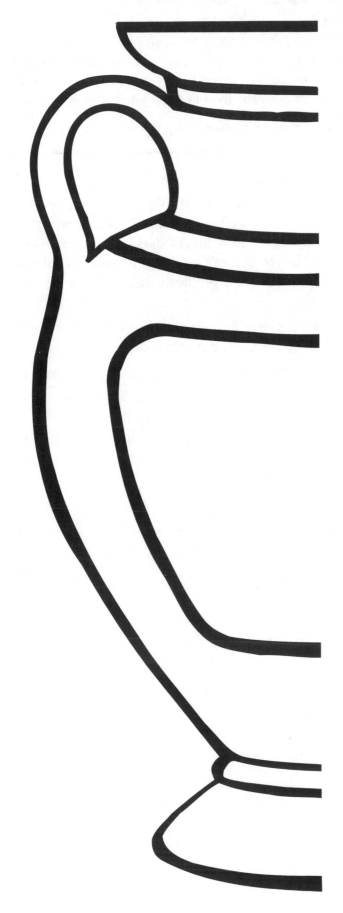

MATERIALS

- 9" x 12" (23 x 30.5 cm) art paper
- watercolor paints
- paintbrush
- pencil
- black marking pen
- paint cloth or newspapers
- pictures of dolphins and fish

FRESCO OF THE SEA

The early Minoans of ancient Greece painted fantastic frescoes on the walls of their palaces. Most Minoan frescoes showed scenes from palace life or nature. Popular frescoes showed women watching a ceremony, games, battles, and life in the sea. The frescoes give archaeologists clues to the lives of these ancient people.

Students create modern frescos using watercolors.

STEPS TO FOLLOW

1. Share the information about the frescoes from page 65 and other resources that are available. Tell students that they will be re-creating a beautiful undersea fresco, such as the one found in a Minoan queen's room in the magnificent palace at Knossos. This fresco showed lively dolphins and fish swimming underwater.

2. Have students sketch lightly with pencil and then paint their underwater scene. Let the painting dry.

3. Instruct students to write the definition of a fresco on the back of their painting.

4. You may choose to make a large fresco (mural) in the classroom using all the students' paintings put together.

Pocket 8

LANGUAGE AND LITERATURE

FAST FACTS

See page 2 for information on how to prepare the Fast Facts bookmark and pocket label. Use the bookmark for a quick review during transition times throughout the day.

ABOUT

Reproduce this page for students. Read about and discuss the language and literature of ancient Greece, highlighting important information to remember. Incorporate library and multimedia resources that are available.

ART REFERENCE

Use this reproducible page as a reference for the activities in the pocket.

ACTIVITIES

The English alphabet is based on the Greek alphabet. After students learn about the Greek alphabet, they write their names using beautiful Greek letters.

Knowing Greek root words can help students understand difficult English words. Students play a dictionary game using Greek root words.

Actors wore two-sided masks that showed two emotions. Students make a two-sided mask to show dramatic and comedic personality traits.

The Greeks loved poetry, especially epics and lyrics. Students write a short lyric poem expressing an emotion.

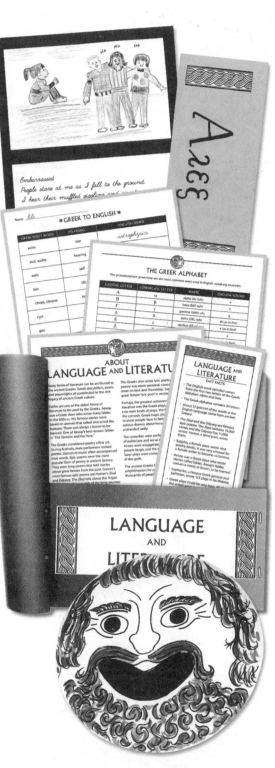

LANGUAGE AND LITERATURE

LANGUAGE AND LITERATURE

FAST FACTS

- The English word *alphabet* comes from the first two letters of the Greek alphabet: *alpha* and *beta*.

- The Greek alphabet contains 24 letters.

- About 12 percent of the words in the English language come from ancient Greece.

- The *Iliad* and the *Odyssey* are famous epic poems. The *Iliad* contains 15,000 verses and the *Odyssey* has 11,000 verses. Homer, a blind poet, wrote them.

- Sappho, a female poet, wrote nine poetry books. It was very unusual for a female writer to become so famous.

- Aesop was a Greek slave who wrote stories called fables. Aesop's fables contain a moral, or lesson, to be learned.

- Sophocles, a famous Greek general and politician, wrote 123 plays in his lifetime.

- Greek plays could be very long. All of the actors were men. They even played the female parts. Each actor played several different parts.

GREEK NAMES

The Greek alphabet letters look somewhat like the English alphabet. Greek alphabet letter names are familiar and still used. The names of college fraternities and sororities are Greek letters. The saying "from alpha to omega," meaning "from beginning to end," is well known.

Students study the Greek alphabet and then compare it to the English one. Then they print their names, calligraphy style, using the Greek alphabet.

STEPS TO FOLLOW

1. Have students read and study the Greek alphabet on page 78.

2. Instruct students to practice writing their names using the Greek alphabet. They will do this by writing it phonetically. They may substitute other Greek letters that are not in the English alphabet to replace missing letters.

3. Direct students to fold the construction paper lengthwise to make a name tag for their desks.

MATERIALS
- page 78, reproduced for each student
- 9" x 12" (23 x 30.5 cm) light-colored construction paper
- writing paper
- calligraphy pen, roller pen, or fine-tipped marking pen
- crayons or marking pens

EXAMPLE

The name Robert, phonetically, is **Rah-bûrt.** The Greek letters you could use would be:

R = rho	**ah = omega**	**t = tau**

Sounds not in the Greek alphabet are "b" and "ûr." You might use **beta**, which has a "v" sound, and **rho** again for "ûr."

Robert would look like this: Ρωβρτ

Their names will not be exactly how the Greeks would have written them, but they will be close.

4. Instruct students to write their Greek name on the name tag using a pen. They should write their English name in a secret place on the name tag too. They may decorate the name tag, if desired.

5. Before putting the name tags in the pocket, collect the name tags and then pass them back out to the class randomly. Have students decode the names and find their rightful owners.

GREEK TO ENGLISH

About 12 percent of all English words come from the ancient Greeks. Knowing Greek root words helps people to understand the meaning of more difficult vocabulary words. For example, putting two Greek root words together can form a whole new word. Here are a couple of examples: *auto* (self) + *graph* (write) = *autograph* (self-writing), *bio* (life) + *logy* (study of) = *biology* (study of life).

Students are given a list of Greek root words to use to play a dictionary game. You may choose to play this word game as a whole class, in small groups, or individually.

MATERIALS

- page 81, reproduced for each student
- pencil
- dictionary for each student

STEPS TO FOLLOW

1. With students, read the Greek root words and meanings on page 81.

2. Tell students that it is their job to fill in the third column with an English word that begins or ends with the Greek root word. They may use a dictionary to help with spelling. For an added challenge, you may want them to write two or more English words and give them a limited time in which to complete the sheet.

3. Make a composite list of all the words students find. Post the list for use as a writing reference. Encourage students to suggest additions to the class list and to add other Greek roots they come across. (Be sure to verify that these additions are Greek, and not Latin.)

POSSIBLE ANSWERS

astro—astronomy, astronaut, astronomical, astral, astrology, astrophysics

aud, audio—audiovisual, audience, auditorium, audition, audible

auto—automobile, autograph, automatic, automation, autoimmune

bio—biology, biography, biopsy, biosphere, biochemistry

chron, chrono—chronology, chronological, chronicle, chronometer, chronic, synchronize

cycl—bicycle, cyclone, cycle, encyclopedia, recycle

geo—geology, geography, geometry, geophysics, geodesic

meter—thermometer, centimeter (etc.), diameter, barometer

micro—microscope, microchip, microscopic, microfilm, microwave, microcosm

mon, mono—monarch, monotone, monotonous, monorail, monopoly, monoplane

phon, phono—phonograph, phonics, microphone, symphony

tele—television, telephone, telegraph, telescope, telethon

EMC 3705 • Ancient Greece • ©2003 by Evan-Moor Corp.

▣ GREEK TO ENGLISH ▣

GREEK ROOT WORD	MEANING	ENGLISH WORD
astro	star	*astrophysics*
aud, audio	hearing	
auto	self	
bio	life	
chron, chrono	time	
cycl	circle	
geo	earth	
meter	to measure	
micro	small	
mon, mono	one	
phon, phono	sound	
tele	far	

THEATER MASKS

Just two or three male actors usually performed Greek plays. Most plays had many parts, so the actors had to switch roles quickly. The actors wore masks made of linen, wood, or leather to help distinguish the different parts they played. The masks also helped the men play female parts since women were not allowed to be actors. The masks had wide-open mouths to allow the voices of the actors to be heard in the large amphitheater that could seat 18,000 spectators. With these large, exaggerated masks, the audience could also tell from far away whether the character was young or old, male or female. Some of the masks were reversible; they had calm expressions on one side and angry ones on the other.

Students make a two-sided mask to show the two sides of a personality in a play.

MATERIALS

- large white paper plate or cardboard circle
- scraps of colored construction paper
- pencil
- fine- and wide-tipped marking pens
- craft materials such as yarn, buttons, and pipe cleaners
- glue

STEPS TO FOLLOW

1. Discuss the information about masks with students. Show pictures of Greek masks, if possible. (An Internet search for Greek masks will turn up lots of samples.)

2. On one side of the paper plate, have students draw a character that has a calm, happy, or comedic expression. Show them how the placement of the eyebrows really makes a difference in a person's expressions.

3. On the other side of the paper plate, have students draw a character that has a serious or angry expression. They should draw the mouth wide open and color it black.

4. Encourage students to add decorations to the masks, for example, yarn for hair and buttons for eyes.

LYRIC POETRY

A lyric poem is a short poem that expresses personal feeling. Lyric poetry may be free verse or may rhyme.

Sappho, the great Greek poet, wrote lyric poetry about love, friendship, and the many different emotions people experience in life. Students write their own poem, emphasizing an emotion.

STEPS TO FOLLOW

1. Define lyric poetry for students.

2. As a class, brainstorm emotions and words that would describe those emotions. You may wish to write a few "feelings" poems together using the following pattern.

Write a feeling on the first line.

> Embarrassed
>
> People stare at me as I fall to the ground.
>
> I hear their muffled giggling and snorting sounds.
>
> My mouth is as dry as cotton and full of dust.
>
> The lump on my head begins to grow,
>
> And my skin feels prickly and cold.
>
> I start to sweat when a friend touches my hand.
>
> She helps me stand, and we walk away in silence.

MATERIALS

- 9" x 12" (23 x 30.5 cm) colored construction paper
- 5" x 8" (13 x 20 cm) writing paper
- 5" x 8" (13 x 20 cm) drawing paper
- pencil
- pen
- crayons or marking pens

Write a line describing that feeling for as many of the five senses as you can—seeing, hearing, tasting, touching, and smelling.

3. Then have students write their own lyric based on an emotion.

4. Direct students to write the final copy of the poem using a pen and then have them illustrate that emotion. Mount the poem and illustration onto colored construction paper. Remind students to pick a color that describes the emotion they wrote about.

Pocket 9
SPORTS AND ENTERTAINMENT

FAST FACTS

See page 2 for information on how to prepare the Fast Facts bookmark and pocket label. Use the bookmark for a quick review during transition times throughout the day.

ABOUT

Reproduce this page for students. Read about and discuss sports and entertainment in ancient Greece, highlighting important information to remember. Incorporate library and multimedia resources that are available.

ART REFERENCE

Use this reproducible page as a reference for the activities in the pocket.

ACTIVITIES

Students make an Olympic torch to use when they say the Olympic oath.

Students report on one of the popular sporting events in the ancient Greek Olympic Games.

EMC 3705 • Ancient Greece • ©2003 by Evan-Moor Corp.

SPORTS AND ENTERTAINMENT

SPORTS AND ENTERTAINMENT
FAST FACTS

- Between 20,000 and 50,000 people traveled to Olympia to watch the Olympic Games.

- Athletes took an Olympic oath in front of the statue of Zeus, swearing they had trained for 10 months and would follow all the rules.

- Olympic athletes were not given cash prizes. The winners did receive money for the return journey home and free meals for life.

- After the Greeks defeated the Persians at the Battle of Marathon, they sent their best runner, Pheidippides, to Athens with the news. He ran 26 miles (42 km) and cried out, "We have won!" And then he dropped dead. That story inspired the modern Olympic event called the marathon.

- Archaeologists uncovered many buildings in Olympia. There were two temples dedicated to Zeus and Hera. Surrounding the temples was a hostel (hotel), restaurants, a huge gymnasium, and a hippodrome (horseracing track).

- Women were banned from competing or even watching the Olympic Games. Women did hold their own games at Olympia in honor of the goddess Hera.

- At banquets called symposia, slaves washed guests' hands and feet before they could enter the party. The slaves also put garlands of leaves or flowers on the guests' heads. Only men attended symposia.

ABOUT
SPORTS AND ENTERTAINMENT

Sports and entertainment were important to the ancient Greeks. Wealthier Greeks had leisure time to spend attending athletic events, going to the gymnasium, giving dinner parties, and participating in special festivals.

The ancient Greeks are especially noted for their great sporting events called the Olympic Games. The first recorded ancient Olympic Games took place in Olympia in 776 B.C. In addition to being an athletic competition, the Olympics were a celebration of the harvest and a religious festival to honor Zeus. The Olympic Games were considered so important that every four years the city-states stopped fighting each other so citizens could compete in or watch the Olympics.

At first the only Olympic event was a 200-yard (183 m) footrace called the stade. Later on, other sporting events were added. Chariot and horse races were held in the hippodrome. The hippodrome was an open-air stadium with a track going

around it. The five-event pentathlon was the most difficult event. Athletes competed in discus and javelin throwing, long jumping, running, and wrestling. Boxing was added to complete the games. The winners of the events were given a wreath of olive branches and the honor of becoming heroes in their own city-states.

When the men were not at the Olympic Games, they could be seen at the gymnasium exercising and talking with their friends. Wealthy men also had the privilege of entertaining guests at a banquet called the symposium. The symposium included serious discussions about politics, but as the evening progressed, men spent more time telling stories, singing, watching entertainers, drinking wine, and eating delicious food.

Men and women were definitely not equal in ancient Greece, but women did have private parties and held their own athletic events. Games were held at Olympia to honor the goddess Hera.

   EMC 3705 • Ancient Greece • ©2003 by Evan-Moor Corp.

THE ANCIENT OLYMPIC GAMES

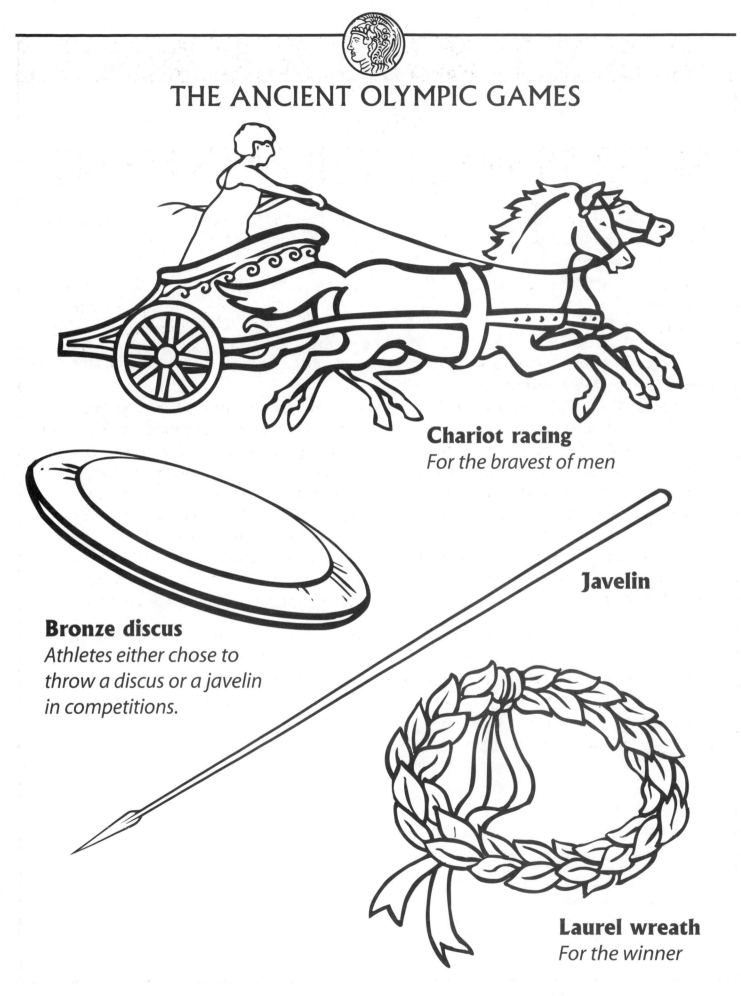

Chariot racing
For the bravest of men

Bronze discus
Athletes either chose to throw a discus or a javelin in competitions.

Javelin

Laurel wreath
For the winner

THE OLYMPIC TORCH

The tradition of the Olympic torch stems from relay races in ancient Greece that were held at night. Students read about and make an Olympic torch, and then read the Olympic oath.

MATERIALS

- page 89 and 90, reproduced for each student
- 9" x 12" (23 x 30.5 cm) black construction paper
- pencil
- scissors
- yellow and orange tempera paint
- small pieces of sponge
- newspaper
- stapler

STEPS TO FOLLOW

1. Discuss the Greek Olympics, comparing it to the modern Olympics. Read the Olympic oath and the information that explains the tradition of the Olympic torch.

2. Have students sponge paint the top of the torch pattern on page 89, using a combination of yellow and orange. Students may sponge over the lines, as the pattern will be cut out.

3. Allow the paint to dry. Then cut out the pattern and glue it to construction paper. Trim the black border around the shape if desired.

4. Cut out the two torch bases on page 90, coloring the cover if desired. Staple them to the torch to create a booklet.

5. Have the students practice reading or memorizing the oath to say as a class.

⊞ THE OLYMPIC TORCH ⊞

THE
OLYMPIC OATH

In the name of all competitors, I promise that we shall take part in these Olympic Games, respecting and abiding by the rules which govern them, in the true spirit of sportsmanship, for the glory of the sport and the honor of our teams.

THE OLYMPIC TORCH

In ancient Greece, relay races with torches took place after dark. The winning team lit a fire on altars to Zeus and Athena. The carrying of the torch became a tradition for the modern Olympic Games. Before the games start, a flaming torch is carried from Athens, Greece, to the host city. The flame may be transported by boat and airplane. Then runners carry the torch across the host country to the games. At the opening ceremony of the Olympic Games, the torch is carried into the stadium and then used to light a larger replica of the smaller torch. Athletes then say the Olympic oath.

OLYMPIC SPORTS

Students pretend they have been admitted into the ancient Greek games to write a sports article for the local paper. Because there are so many events going on in the stadium, the students have to choose one of the four events to write about.

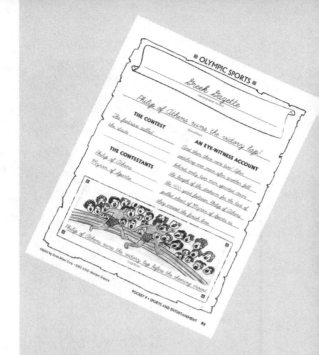

STEPS TO FOLLOW

1. Have students read about the sporting events on page 92. Instruct them to choose one of those events to report on for a local newspaper. Have students research further information about the sport, using other references if available.

2. After the students have researched the event, have them write a news article using the form on page 93. They are to create a headline and write a report as if they had viewed the event at Olympia. They include a picture and a caption to go with the article.

3. Instruct students to create a name for their "newspaper"— *Olympic Orator, Greek Gazette, Marathon Mirror*—and write it in the banner at the top of the page.

4. Encourage students to share their articles with the class.

5. As an extension activity, students could pretend they are sportscasters and give the class a play-by-play description of the action.

MATERIALS

- pages 92 and 93, reproduced for each student
- pencil

OLYMPIC SPORTS

FOOTRACE

The footrace was called the stade. Athletes sprinted 400 yards (366 m) up and down the length of the stadium. That means the runner ended up sprinting for about 3 miles (5 km). The runners could be disqualified if they cut in front of, tripped, or elbowed other runners.

WRESTLING

Two men wrestled until one wrestler threw his opponent to the ground three times. This could take hours to achieve. The match could also end if one of the men was too injured to continue. Gouging and biting disqualified the wrestlers.

LONG JUMPING

Long jumpers carried heavy weights to give them more momentum when they took off. They jumped on a bed of smoothly raked, crumbled earth. This left clear footprints so the judges could measure the distance each man jumped. A long jumper was disqualified if he tried to inch forward once he had landed.

JAVELIN OR DISCUS THROWING

Athletes chose to throw either a javelin, which is a long pole, or a bronze discus. The athletes had to find the best throwing angle and know exactly when to let go of the javelin or discus. An athlete could be disqualified if he stepped over the starting mark when throwing.

EMC 3705 • Ancient Greece • ©2003 by Evan-Moor Corp.

Name: _____

⊞ OLYMPIC SPORTS ⊞

_____
(newspaper name)

_____
(headline)

THE CONTEST

_____

_____

_____

THE CONTESTANTS

_____

_____

AN EYE-WITNESS ACCOUNT

_____

_____

_____

_____

_____

_____

_____
(caption)

TRIVIA OF ANCIENT GREECE

Students create four trivia cards about ancient Greece, and then quiz each other.

STEPS TO FOLLOW

1. Encourage students to reread their pockets. They choose four facts they learned to use as the basis for their trivia questions.

2. Students write four questions, one per index card. They may choose from three types of questions: multiple choice, fill in the blank, or open-ended. For multiple-choice questions, they should include three choices numbered 1, 2, and 3.

3. Students write the answers to each of their questions on the backs of the four index cards.

4. Students pair up and quiz one another with their cards.

5. Students punch holes in cards and attach with a metal ring. Store trivia cards in Pocket 1.

6. Optional:

   • Once all questions are asked, take a survey about the subjects used. Make a tally list on the board to see what subjects seemed to interest students the most.

   • To ensure more complete coverage of topics, you might assign a specific pocket to each small group of 2 to 4 students, ensuring that all topics will be addressed.

   • Make copies of all questions and create a class trivia game, complete with board.

MATERIALS

• four 3" x 5" (7.5 x 13 cm) index cards

• pencil

• scissors

• transparent tape

• hole punch

• metal ring

• Optional: crayons or marking pens

EMC 3705 • Ancient Greece • ©2003 by Evan-Moor Corp.

ANCIENT GREECE—REFLECTION SHEET

Name: _____ Date: _____

Directions: Please fill out this sheet after you have completed the Ancient Greece book. Place your reflection sheet in the first pocket.

1. When I look through my Ancient Greece book, I feel _____

   because _____

   _____

2. The project I liked doing the most was the _____

   because _____

   _____

3. The project I liked doing the least was the _____

   because _____

   _____

4. Three things I am most proud of in my Ancient Greece book are _____

   _____

   _____

   _____

5. Three things I would do differently to improve my Ancient Greece book are _____

   _____

   _____

   _____

6. Three facts that I learned about ancient Greece that I did not know before doing this project are

   _____

   _____

   _____

7. Name three achievements or inventions of the ancient Greeks. How has each of these achievements or inventions affected our lives today?

   _____

   _____

   _____

ANCIENT GREECE—EVALUATION SHEET

Directions: Look through all the pockets and evaluate how well the activities were completed. Use the following point system:

6 outstanding	5 excellent	4 very good	3 satisfactory	2 some effort	1 little effort	0 no effort

Self-Evaluation	Peer Evaluation	Teacher Evaluation
Name: _____	Name: _____	____ completed assignments
____ completed assignments	____ completed assignments	____ followed directions
____ followed directions	____ followed directions	____ had correct information
____ had correct information	____ had correct information	____ edited writing
____ edited writing	____ edited writing	____ showed creativity
____ showed creativity	____ showed creativity	____ displayed neatness
____ displayed neatness	____ displayed neatness	____ added color
____ added color	____ added color	____ **total points**
____ **total points**	____ **total points**	____ **grade**
Comments: _____	Comments: _____	Comments: _____

EMC 3705 • Ancient Greece •©2003 by Evan-Moor Corp.